Praise for *Curious*

'There is something of the cool aunt about Rebecca Front. As an actress, she is both mumsy and quietly subversive. She's equally at ease collaborating with Steve Coogan and Armando Iannucci as she is in cosy crime such as *Midsomer Murders* and *Lewis*. The one constant is an eyebrow arched high. This winning delivery comes across in *Curious*, in which she mixes autobiography with baffled rant. And like her screen persona, her writing is funny and touching' *Daily Telegraph*

'Both original and entertaining' Viv Groskop, *Sunday Express*

'Rebecca . . . has anxieties to burn, and writes amusingly and perceptively about them' Markus Berkmann, *Daily Mail*

'Actress Rebecca Front offers not a straight autobiography but a string of quirky stories, memories and personal anxieties'
Mail on Sunday

'Rebecca Front is an award-winning actress from TV political satire *The Thick of It* and also, it turns, out a brilliant story-teller. She's written for the *Guardian* and the *Independent* for years and *Curious* is her first book. Sharp, funny and often poignant, it is a collection of witty stories and sketches from her own life' *Good Housekeeping*

'A brilliant storyteller, it's the curious in the quotidian that attracts her gaze as she spins her funny and poignant tales'
Scotsman

'Rebecca Front's playful observations about the remarkable and curious moments in everyday life meant that I read her book with a frequent smile on my face. There's an

Alice-in-Wonderland charm to the writing, and the stories range from the uninvited guest who sets up home in the family living room to a witty analysis of celebrity hierarchy. It's the kind of book where certain insights and experiences stick with you – you want to tuck them safely away so you can draw on them when you need them' *Psychologies* magazine

'As you might expect from an actress who made her name in such darkly comic TV series as *The Thick of It* and *Nighty Night*, Rebecca Front tells a very funny tale. Her debut book is a gloriously entertaining collection of personal stories and anecdotes from her childhood to the present day'   *Hello!*

'Rebecca Front proves herself to be an entertaining raconteur, mixing personal reminiscences with unusual observations of everyday life'   *Choice*

Rebecca Front is a BAFTA-winning actress and writer. She is perhaps best known for her work in television comedy series such as *The Thick of It*, *The Day Today*, *Knowing Me, Knowing You with Alan Partridge*, *Nighty Night* and *Psychobitches*, as well as such dramas as *Lewis* and *Death Comes to Pemberley*. She has also written extensively. Her columns have often appeared in the *Guardian*, *Independent* and many other publications. With her brother Jeremy, she writes and stars in BBC Radio 4's *Incredible Women*. Born in east London, she read English at St Hugh's College, Oxford, and was the first female president of the Oxford Revue.

@RebeccaFront

For my children:
They already have all my heart,
but they might like to have this too.

CURIOUS

True Stories and Everyday Absurdities

REBECCA FRONT

WEIDENFELD & NICOLSON

A W&N PAPERBACK

First published in Great Britain in 2014
by Weidenfeld & Nicolson
This paperback edition published in 2015
by Weidenfeld & Nicolson,
an imprint of Orion Books Ltd,
Carmelite House, 50 Victoria Embankment,
London EC4Y 0DZ

An Hachette UK company

1 3 5 7 9 10 8 6 4 2

Copyright © Rebecca Front 2014

The right of Rebecca Front to be identified as the author of
this work has been asserted by her in accordance with the
Copyright, Designs and Patents Act 1988.

A CIP catalogue record for this book
is available from the British Library.

ISBN 978-1-7802-2611-8

Printed and bound in Great Britain by CPI Group (UK) Ltd, Croydon, CR0 4YY

The Orion Publishing Group's policy is to use papers that
are natural, renewable and recyclable products and
made from wood grown in sustainable forests. The logging
and manufacturing processes are expected to conform to
the environmental regulations of the country of origin.

www.orionbooks.co.uk

Contents

Prologue

The night the earthquake struck in Dudley, my four-year-old son had a fever. He was in bed with me, so that I could keep a close eye on him. Some time around midnight, he'd awoken, coughing and sweating. His eyes were glazed, probably because he was still half asleep, but I couldn't be sure. Fevers and small children are a volatile mix – all the literature said so. They can take a downward turn alarmingly quickly. You had to look for 'signs' – rashes, shortness of breath, delirium. I was barely awake myself, and not at all sure I was up to the job.

I tried to get him to drink some water, but he pushed the cup away, looked at me and said, 'Who are you?'

This wasn't good.

It was dark in the room – could it just be that?

Perhaps my work–life balance had been so out of whack that week that he genuinely couldn't place me.

Or was it – something worse?

My mind began racing through a montage of disaster scenarios: an ambulance being called; a doctor berating me for not bringing my child in sooner, shouting, 'He asked you who you were and it didn't ring alarm bells?' and me whimpering, 'You don't understand, I appear in niche comedy shows, I'm used to not being recognised.'

My son was still drowsily coughing in my arms, so I asked him 'Do you know who *you* are?' trying to keep the rising panic out of my voice. He didn't answer – but then it was quite a metaphysical question for a four-year-old.

'What's your name?' I offered as a simpler alternative.

He looked at me with a faint smile, and said, 'I'm Gary the Snail.'

I ran into the spare room to where Phil had been relegated. 'We need to get him to hospital,' I said.

'He's got a cough, Bec.'

'He thinks he's a snail.'

Phil followed me into the darkened bedroom and stroked our son's face to wake him up again.

'You OK, mate?' he whispered.

'Yup.'

'Do you want some water?'

'Yup.'

He seemed to be reserving the delirium for me.

'Who's Gary the Snail?' I asked.

'SpongeBob's pet,' he said with a grin. Then he sipped some water and went back to sleep. *SpongeBob SquarePants* – his favourite show. He wasn't hallucinating, he was trying to make me laugh.

'OK, I may have overreacted,' I whispered to Phil, but he just looked at me blankly, rubbed his eyes and wandered back to the spare bed.

I lay down next to my sleeping boy and dozed off myself. Something woke me – it felt like only moments later – and I thought he must have fallen off the bed. But he was still there, in exactly the same position, quietly snoring.

As I became more conscious, I realised that what I'd heard hadn't been a bang or a thud – in fact I didn't quite know what it was. Nothing had fallen from any of the shelves, the pictures were still on the walls. I couldn't fathom it at all.

Sometimes things are much more ordinary than you think, like my son's 'hallucination' being nothing more than a little boy's idea of funny. And sometimes they're a whole lot odder than you can possibly imagine, like the fact that an earthquake had struck the West Midlands. As soon as I saw it on the news, I knew that's what I'd heard. It wasn't even really a sound at all. It was a shifting, a sensation, an awareness that something wasn't right.

Both events – the sick child and the tremor – were simultaneously normal and abnormal, natural and unnatural, perfectly all right and worryingly wrong. And that's the spectrum we exist on, that's everyday life: part seismic activity, part misplaced joke.

The stories that follow are about such curiosities – the awkwardness of human interaction, the unshakeability of fear, the randomness of memories. Being curious was my starting point, in both the active sense – being interested in people and things; and the passive – being, as we all are, a bit odd.

All of them are true, though perhaps a little bent out of shape in the telling. They are about the strangeness that fascinates me in myself, in others and (if you'll forgive the assumption) in you. There are character studies and observations, memories and digressions; singular events dealt with in a matter-of-fact fashion, and quotidian events never really dealt with at all.

If you recognise something of yourself in here, then great. If, on the other hand, it just confirms that yours is the only sane voice in an otherwise bonkers world, then that's fine too. You might want to get a little expert help with that, but it's fine nonetheless.

This is a book of curiosities; and if you're curious enough to read on – I thank you, and hope it reminds you of curiosities of your own.

The tiger who came to tea

Shortly before my brother's bar mitzvah, a stranger took over our home. We didn't exactly invite him; we didn't exactly block his way. He just quietly invaded, conquered us by stealth, and his greatest weapon was our own stupid politeness.

My dad had an uncle called Merv. There were uncles and cousins scattered all over the place, most of whom were just names to us, but Merv, who lived in Miami, had visited London several years earlier and made quite an impression. Many of Dad's relatives reminded me faintly of American stars. Even though both parents came from immigrant stock, Mum's family were somehow terribly English, rather shy and eager to blend in, while Dad's were all larger-than-life. There was an aunt who was a bit like Ethel Merman married to an uncle who had a touch of Eddie Cantor. Merv, when he visited, was somewhere between Lou Costello and Ernest Borgnine, and looked like such a quintessential American tourist that we felt like we'd known him all our lives, whereas in fact we'd just seen characters like him on TV. He was loud and funny and peppered the conversation with phrases like 'honest to god' and 'you gotta be kidding'. Like my dad's father, Merv owned a barber shop, so he was full of gags and banter and made conversation as easily as breathing. By the time he went back to Miami, he'd already become a favourite.

Transatlantic phone calls in those days were expensive and often afflicted with time delays and inaudibility. The upside to this was that when Merv and Dad had their occasional catch-ups, both had to shout to be heard, and Jeremy and I could sit on the stairs and listen to them shooting the breeze.

And that was how we first heard about Bob.

'Listen, Charlie,' Merv was yelling across four thousand miles of airspace, 'This fella walked into my shop the other day, nice guy, a photographer. So I'm cutting his hair, not that anyone wants much off these days ... everyone's a hippy like you ... but I says to him, funny thing, I got a nephew who's an artist in London.'

'I'm not a hippy, Merv. But now I don't have to work in an office, why do I need a short back and sides?'

'You look how you wanna look, Charlie,' Merv yelled, indulgently. '*Gesundheit*. As long as you got your strength. Anyway, so this fella, the photographer, his name is Bob Lerman. And I says to him you should look my nephew up, I think you'd get along.'

'He's coming to London?' asked Dad.

'Sure, he's going to *Europe*. The whole of *Europe*. He's gonna take photographs, maybe get a little work. I've given him your number.'

From my vantage point on the top landing, I could see Dad tensing a little. It wasn't that he and Mum were inhospitable, just that unlike Merv they didn't become firm friends with people on first meeting. They liked to build up to it gradually, keep a little distance, take it one step at a time. But if Merv had given our phone number to this totally unknown hippy photographer, they would have to be welcoming – take him out for a drink, maybe buy him dinner. In a moment of breezy camaraderie, Merv had landed Dad with a new 'friend' on the flimsy premise that they both had collar-length hair.

'Now as a matter of fact, Charlie,' Merv continued, 'Bob thinks you could do him a little favour. He's gotta have some paperwork signed ... I dunno, some kind of permit ... and he needs a UK resident to sign it. Like a sponsorship thing ... whatever.'

By now my mum had come out into the hallway and was mouthing, 'Don't sign ANYTHING.'

'Right ...' said Dad, uncertainly.

'I mean it's just a form, you know? Not like a contract or anything legal. Just to say you know this guy ...'

'Well ... I *don't*, of course,' protested Dad, trying to keep a smile in his voice, while mouthing back at my mother, 'I'm not STUPID, Sheila.'

'Listen, you'll meet him, you'll love him. Then all you gotta say is ... he's legit ... he won't outstay his welcome. You're OK with that, right?'

'Well, you know ... we'll see how it goes,' said Dad, and gestured to my mother triumphantly as if to say, 'There, I haven't committed us to anything.' But she just glared at him and went back into the living room. She knew he was about to be bulldozed.

'Terrific, I already told him you'd do it,' said Merv.

'OK,' sighed Dad. And even though I couldn't see her, I knew Mum was sitting, pursed-lipped and fuming, waiting for him to get off the phone.

For some weeks, we heard nothing. The whole household was absorbed in Jeremy's forthcoming bar mitzvah – a bit like planning for a wedding but without the element of anyone actually looking forward to it. Jeremy was nervously rehearsing his parsha – the long passage of Hebrew he would have to recite in front of the entire congregation. Mum and Dad were up to their eyes in table plans and speeches and conversations with the caterer about vol au vents. Because the whole thing, modest though it was, was inevitably going to cost more money than they could comfortably afford, they'd tried to mitigate the expense by having the kiddush – the little drinks celebration straight after the service and before the dinner/dance – at our house. But in saving the cost of hiring the synagogue hall, they'd landed themselves with a whole lot of additional work. Both house and garden, though they looked fine to me, apparently needed radical work to make them presentable, and without the luxury of a cleaner or gardener, we had to do it all ourselves.

So it was that Dad and I were out in the front garden one Saturday afternoon, trying somewhat ineptly to wrestle the holly bush into topiary form, when Mum came to the front door and announced there was someone called Bob on the phone. Dad disappeared for a few moments, and Mum came out to be with me. I was nine and very sensible, but she could always see the danger lurking in apparently harmless scenarios, so leaving me alone with a pair of shears was never going to happen. Unfortunately, in avoiding this remote risk, she had overlooked the greater one of leaving my dad unattended on the phone. When he returned, he looked a little sheepish.

'I'm going to pick him up,' he said flatly, as though he'd just been sideswiped by a large, unseen vehicle.

'Who?'

'Bob Lerman.'

'Who's Bob Lerman?'

'Uncle Merv's friend,' I explained, to speed things along a bit.

'You're going to pick him up? Where from?'

'Heathrow,' said Dad.

'You don't even know him,' said Mum. She'd gone a bit shrill. I took the shears off her.

'He said he'll be wearing a fishing hat.'

'I'm not worried about how you're going to recognise him. I'm worried about why you're schlepping right across London to pick up a guy you've never met, just because he once had a trim at your uncle's barber shop. And where are you taking him?'

Apparently Bob had had the foresight to check himself into a hotel in Kensington, but not to figure out how to get there on public transport. Or in a taxi. Even at the age of nine, I wondered how he was going to make it round the whole of Europe. Dad had known, the instant he'd got off the phone, that *he* and not Bob was the one being taken for a ride, but a promise is a promise, so off he went. As he drove away, Mum called after him, 'Don't bring him here. And DON'T SIGN ANYTHING.'

It was no surprise to any of us that when Dad returned a few hours later, the passenger seat was occupied by a guy in a fishing hat. Mum uttered a few *sotto voce* expletives, then framed her face into a welcoming smile and opened the front door.

Bob got out of the car first, and walked towards Mum with an outstretched hand:

'You must be Sheila. Bob. Bob Lerman.'

Mum went to take his hand and instead found herself locked in a bear hug. This went on just long enough for her entire torso to stiffen with embarrassment, at which point Bob released her, then instantly gripped her anew by both shoulders, stared into her face and said, 'Thank you for welcoming me into your home, Sheila.' Mum nodded, accidentally implying assent, and Bob pushed past her into the house.

'Why is he here?' she asked Dad in a whisper, furious but too polite to let Bob know it.

'I honestly don't know, Sheila. I took him to the hotel and they ... there was some mix-up ... and he's got all this camera equipment ... it's worth thousands of dollars, so he couldn't go to a youth hostel ... and he asked me to take care of the stuff and suddenly I'd agreed to bring him here.' And as if to prove how bewildered he was, Dad had by now carried all Bob's luggage into the hall himself, without Bob even offering to help.

Mum made tea and Bob waited for her to sit down with hers before saying he'd rather have coffee. Then we all sat around in the front room trying to get the measure of this strange arrival. He'd taken off the fishing hat now, but was still dressed in head-to-toe khaki as if ready for combat. He was tall and thin, a little feeble looking, but with alert, beady eyes. His hair was long and straggly and he had a wispy, insubstantial beard. He wasn't, it had to be said, a great advertisement for Merv's barbering skills. His skin was pale and covered in angry eczematous blotches. Everything about him both screamed that he needed looking after, and made you not want to be the one to do it.

Jeremy and I usually enjoyed it when people came round – it broke up the everydayness of family life, and made us all behave like heightened versions of ourselves. Dad would be jokier than usual, Mum more charming. There were endless offerings of food and drink and small talk. All of this happened now, but Bob seemed impervious to it. He wasn't actually rude or impolite, but he saw no need to pretend that this was anything other than a straightforward parasitic coupling. His presence among us was functional – he needed shelter, we could provide it. We were the hosts he was going to feed off.

It may have been an unintended consequence of this aloof-ness – though nonetheless a useful one for him – that the less *he* tried, the more *we* did. The rules of polite society are so deeply ingrained in us that even if a guest is unwelcome, you somehow have to make them feel at home. The more you wish someone wasn't there, the more you feel the need to make them stay. When the last guest at a dinner party finally yawns, stretches and apologises for keeping you up so late, good manners dictate that you pretend not to have noticed the time and offer them a final nightcap. Don't you? Well, that's what my family always did, and Bob must have known pretty quickly that if he'd wanted people to take advantage of, he'd come to the right place.

'So we can't offer you luxury, I'm afraid,' Dad explained, pausing momentarily in case Bob chose to tell us we had a lovely home. He didn't, so Dad carried on. 'We haven't even got a spare room, but you're welcome to sleep on the settee tonight, and in the morning we'll get you checked into a hotel.'

'OK,' said Bob in earnest acknowledgement that he understood, but with no suggestion of gratitude.

'We're vegetarian, by the way,' Mum apologised, implying that if Bob had a problem with this, we might be persuaded to reconsider. He didn't object, but as Mum stood up to head for the kitchen he threw an unexpected curveball.

'I have a condition, kind of a blood glucose thing. I have to eat every three hours, day and night. Otherwise, I may slip into a coma.'

'Gosh. How awful. Day and night? Well, yes … of course … we'll make sure you have plenty of snacks.'

'And I have to sleep for at least ten hours. Uninterrupted.'

Had we been more mathematically minded, we might have wondered how a man could sleep uninterrupted for ten hours while still eating something every three. But instead we just sat there wrestling with the simpler equation that a stranger sleeping in your living room equalled no telly.

'Plus sometimes I just need time alone.'

This was bluntness on an unprecedented scale.

'In addition to the ten hours when you'll be sleeping?' asked Dad.

'Oh yeah. Waking solitude is vital. We all need it. All of us. We gotta have time to "be".'

Mum decided it was now time to 'be' in a room that wasn't full of Bob Lerman, and went to make a start on the first of the many meals she would be preparing that night.

When we got up the next morning, Bob was still asleep. At least the front room door was closed, but he could have just been indulging in a little 'waking solitude'. Either way, since the dining room – which had anyway become Dad's studio years earlier – had been temporarily filled with Bob's ludicrous amount of luggage, we all had to eat breakfast standing up in our little kitchen. Holding our toast and whispering, for fear of interrupting Bob's all-important 'be-time', it felt like we were guests at a particularly disappointing party. Jeremy and I had to go off to Sunday morning Hebrew classes, but we were assured by Mum and Dad that when we got home, Bob would have gone, and we'd have our telly, our eating space and our normal lives back.

But no. He was still there at lunchtime, and dinnertime too. Apparently, there'd been a mix-up over the money he'd allocated for his hotel expenses. I didn't fully understand, but the upshot was that if he could stay just one more night with us, then he'd be able to move in with a friend for a few days. We all assumed that 'friend' was Bob-speak for 'gullible stranger', but frankly we didn't care. Sunday night passed, as Saturday had, with no TV and nowhere to sit comfortably. On Monday morning, after another upright, crowded-into-the-kitchen, buffet breakfast, Jeremy and I went off to school, shouting goodbye to Bob through the closed front room door for what we hoped would be the last time.

He was still there that evening too. He'd had a migraine, apparently worse than any migraine previously known to medical science, and being unable to speak or hear, he naturally couldn't contact his 'friend'. Thus, he had missed the one-day-only opportunity of a cheap place to stay.

And so it went on, day after day after day. There was always another reason why he couldn't leave, always an answer to my parents' objections – he was ill or he was broke; he was scared of something or someone, or he had to wait until a complex set of circumstances came into play. Mum and Dad were simply at a loss as to how to handle him. They'd talk to friends and among themselves and resolve that tomorrow they were going to tell him 'definitely this' or 'no option but that', but he could negotiate his way out of everything; he was utterly impervious to hints, jokes and even outright criticism. He was thick-skinned, smart and ruthless, and my parents slowly (*too* slowly) discovered that what they'd always assumed to be their greatest asset was in fact their fatal flaw – they were just too damned nice.

And there was another reason that they couldn't get tough with him. My mum, a highly intelligent woman, was nonetheless terribly superstitious. She claimed this was as a result of being half-Jewish and half-Welsh, and certainly both my Jewish grandmother and my Welsh one were endlessly skirting round ladders and pretending to spit into 'the evil eye'. To this day my mother sometimes recalls, in an awed tone, how when she was pregnant with me a woman had come to the door selling lucky heather and offering to tell Mum's fortune. Fearful of bringing some curse upon the household, Mum paid her an amount which might reasonably have purchased an entire moorland of traditional, non-lucky heather, whereupon the woman prophesied that she would have a little girl who would grow up to be a dancer. Well she did have a little girl – there was a fifty per cent chance that would come true. But even by the most generous assessment, the dancer part was crazily wide of the mark. And yet every time I passed a tap exam or appeared in a musical, Mum would nod sagely and say there were more things in heaven and earth etc. Perhaps, like all good con-men, Bob had picked up on this, or perhaps he'd just taken a lucky punt, but one day, over one of his three-hourly meals, he casually dropped a bombshell.

'My wife, by the way, wanted me to thank you personally for the way you've taken care of me.'

Mum, still clinging to her rock of politeness, refrained from saying, 'Your *wife*? You have a *wife*?' and plumped instead for, 'Oh ... we didn't realise you were married.'

'Oh yes,' said Bob, 'to Morgan. We're very much in love.'

Dad, suddenly realising that Bob, on top of everything else, had probably been making transatlantic calls without asking, chanced his arm with a 'surely you must be missing her, wouldn't you like to go home?' jibe, but it rolled off Bob's back without a trace.

'She's in college. Completing her studies,' he continued.

'Into what?' Dad asked.

'Witchcraft,' said Bob earnestly, and Mum swallowed hard and pushed away the rest of her sandwich.

From that moment on, all Dad's suggestions for how to get Bob out of the house were met with a quivering rebuttal from Mum on the basis that if we messed with Bob, Morgan might wreak some long-distance occult revenge.

'We could change the locks ...'

'His wife's a witch.'

'We could take out a loan and buy him a plane ticket ...'

'His wife's a witch.'

'We could stop feeding him for a few hours and let the hospital deal with him ...'

'I don't happen to find that kind of remark funny, Charlie. And what if she knows what we're saying?'

'That's just mad.'

'I'll tell you what's mad: you inviting a crazy guy into our home with stinking feet, a permanently empty stomach, and a wife back home with a sodding cauldron.'

And so, for several weeks, things settled into a peculiar kind of normal: Jeremy still had a bar mitzvah coming up, I still went to school, Mum went to work and looked after the parts of the house she could get into, and Dad tried to carry on painting in the little bit of studio that Bob hadn't commandeered for his equipment. It was as if they'd given up fighting him. Nothing had worked, so they'd adjusted to this new reality as helplessly if it were a dream. It's a hard thing to understand now, but it made sense at the time.

When, many years later, my own children were at primary school, there were frequent outbreaks of head lice. Every time it happened, I'd diligently treat them with whatever seemed effective and send them back in nit-free. But because not everyone was quite as scrupulous, they'd come back home with another infestation, and we'd do the whole routine again. And after a while, I can remember thinking: what if I don't bother? Why spend another miserable evening scraping their scalps with combs and dousing them in aesthetically repackaged sheep dip, when I know that ultimately the nits will crawl back in? Maybe we should just accept that they've won; after all, I get the whole child, the nits only get the scalp. Maybe we should just give them their little bit of conquered land. I never did give up, of course. I went on fighting and dousing and combing until the little sods finally caved in and we won.

But that feeling of resignation and exhaustion must have been what had overtaken Mum and Dad; he's won, the front room's his. Just let him have it and we can all get on with our lives.

It was almost a month before the final showdown came. Dad and Jeremy were out, Mum and I were in the kitchen and Bob wandered in looking for yet more food.

'Hey, Sheila,' he remarked, looking at Mum with his head to one side, as if she were a scientific specimen, 'are you OK? You seem a little tense.'

Mum stared at him blankly for a moment, and I honestly thought she was going to say, 'Are you kidding me? YES I'm tense. You've taken over my house.' But she didn't. She just rubbed her eyes and said, 'Well, I've got a lot on my mind.'

'Like what?' asked Bob, sounding almost like someone who gave a shit.

'Well ... you know ... the bar mitzvah, and ... work,' she said, and then gingerly added, 'And you.'

Bob moved towards her and placed his hand on her forehead.

'I'm going to put my karma into you ...' he began. But before he could put *anything* into her, Mum had grabbed me by the hand and picked up her bag and we'd gone. We walked very fast round to Auntie Deena's house, where Mum drank some brandy and Deena told her what she already knew: Bob had to go.

Later that afternoon, while Bob was taking time to 'be' in our front room, Dad quietly and determinedly loaded the thousands of dollars' worth of camera equipment and the many, mysterious bags into the car boot. Then he walked into Bob's room, our living room as it had once been, and stood there, beady eyed and barely containing his rage.

'Time to go, Bob.'

'Uh, well, Charlie, that friend of mine, the one with the room? He's going to be back in London from tomorrow, so if I could just stay here one more ...'

'Time to go. Now. Come on. Enough is enough. You're scaring my wife, you're upsetting my kids. It's time to go.'

'Listen, Charlie. I dunno why it has to be like this. I mean, you're a cool guy, I respect you, and ...'

'Now. Get in the car, please.'

And slowly, reluctantly, and with an elaborate dumb show of bafflement, Bob gathered his few remaining belongings and followed Dad out of the house.

Mum threw open the windows to clear the stench, both literal and metaphorical, that he'd left behind. And then we waited. None of us quite believed that Dad would return alone.

But he did. He'd driven Bob to a small, cheap, commercial hotel just far enough away for him not to be able to find his way back. Bob had protested the whole way that Dad was being unreasonable, inhospitable; that he didn't know what his problem was. He'd even complained that he hadn't signed his form – the one vouching that he was a nice guy who wouldn't outstay his welcome. You had to give him full marks for chutzpah.

When they arrived, Dad checked with the receptionist that they definitely had a room, and took the endless bags into the foyer. Bob, finally defeated, followed him in.

Then Dad said, 'Goodbye, Bob,' got back in the car, and drove all the way home grinning from ear to ear.

That night, we sat in *our* front room, eating *our* dinner in front of *our* telly. Just the four of us, taking time to 'be', enjoying our waking solitude. Bob was right; it suddenly felt really important.

A month or so later, Merv rang for a chat.

'Listen, Merv,' called my dad across the Atlantic, 'do me a favour. Don't send me any more of your clients.'

Merv had no recollection of giving Bob our phone number. At first, he had no recollection of Bob. The whole encounter had been so casual for him and so momentous for us. Finally, after much prompting, it came back to him.

'Oh *Bob*. The photographer guy. Yeah. Nice fella. Haven't seen him in a while. I think he went to Europe.'

'He came here. To London. He stayed in our house for a month.'

'A month? Boy, you two must have really hit it off.'

Dad laughed bitterly. 'No, Merv. We really didn't. He's a taker, a con-man. We couldn't get him to leave.'

Merv hooted with disbelief.

'Whaddya mean, you couldn't get him to leave? Why didn't you just tell him where to get off? Kick his ass outta there? Give the guy hell?'

Dad was momentarily lost for words. From my vantage point on the top stair, I could see him considering all of these suggestions. They sounded so simple, and it suddenly dawned on him that he could have done that right from the start. Why had he let this stranger take over his home, upset his family, eat his food, take him for a ride? Why hadn't he, when it sounded so simple, told him where to get off?

'Because ...' he began trying to articulate, 'well ... because ...'

Why had it been so difficult? He was waving one arm at the unseen Merv, trying to reach for a plausible explanation, trying to understand it himself. Finally, there it was – the simple truth.

'Because I'm English.'

Out of my depth

It's not that I don't like the idea of floating. I can see the appeal of just lying there, letting the water hold me, playing fast and loose with gravity; only I'd rather it was on my terms. When I want to stop floating, then I want to stop floating now. Not when I get to the side of the pool, but now. And it doesn't work like that, does it? Not when you're out of your depth. I need to learn to trust the water to support me. And I do. Well, I don't, but I will. Won't I? Of course I will.

'Of course'; your phrase, not mine. There's no of course about it, in my mind. I've never trusted water, and I doubt that that will change. But I'm here, and I'm trying, though frankly I don't know why. You're still holding on to me, aren't you? God, now I don't trust you either.

It's my fourth lesson and I'm still terrified. Terrified. My heart's pounding, and I'm sweating *and* shivering, and I keep forgetting to breathe out. Not forgetting. I'm scared to breathe out. Because while my lungs are inflated like balloons, then logic – my logic, which I accept is not what most people might actually *call* logic – tells me that I stand more of a chance of staying afloat. Once the air goes out, I'll sink. Won't I? 'Of course I will'; my phrase this time. But I mean, it stands to reason. So I'm holding the air in for as long as I can, no matter how often you tell me to trust the water, because I don't trust the water, and I don't trust you, and I wish I'd never come to this chlorinated, condensated hell-hole. Not that I'll ever tell you that, of course. I'm far too polite, and it's not your fault I can't swim. You're trying your hardest to help, but it's all just a bit too late.

I will have a go in a minute. I'm bracing myself ... well, the opposite really. Relaxing myself. Trying to. I used to have this self-help tape that said, 'It's impossible to have a panic attack if every muscle in your body is relaxed.' I loved that. The man's voice was completely reassuring and authoritative, and I'd listen to him and think, 'That's it then.' That's the answer. That's all I have to do. And then one day I realised that if you turned the words around and got the same confident voice to say them – 'It's impossible to relax every muscle in your body if you're having a panic attack' – then that would be true too. I lost faith in self-help after that.

Right, maybe you could just let go for a second ... not yet, but on the count of three. Deep breath. I shouldn't have mentioned the word 'deep'. How deep is the water here? No, it doesn't matter, don't tell me. It's better if I don't think about it. OK. Here we go. In a second. Not quite yet. OK. One, two, three ...

One bright summer's day, sitting on a riverbank, I watched my father drowning. I was with my mum, finishing off a cheese and mustard sandwich while she packed away the picnic detritus. My dad and my brother were paddling, nothing more. Dad couldn't swim, just like he couldn't ride a bike. As a child, he'd been accident prone, so to keep him from danger, his mother had stopped him learning to do risky things. If he couldn't ride a bike, he couldn't fall off. If he couldn't swim, he wouldn't drown. There was a beguiling charm to the illogicality of it. He'd been obedient all his life, and even now in his forties, he was doing nothing more dangerous than paddling with his teenage son on the hottest day of the year. Fate's idea of a joke, I suppose.

'They're waving,' my mum said. And we waved back, half-wondering why we were bothering when they'd only gone a hundred yards or so. They were right by the bank. I could see them. At least I could see my brother, still waving but more urgently now, and shouting something. 'He must know we can't hear him,' I thought. But he carried on, and soon there were other voices shouting too, and my mother stood up and started to run.

I can remember cutting my bare foot on a rock, seeing blood on the grass, but it didn't hurt and it didn't matter, so I carried on running. I caught up with my mum and I heard her calling in a hollow, frightened voice, 'Is he all right?' My brother was standing there, dripping, and looking down at this shape on the ground. There were onlookers, some of them wet from having waded in to help pull him out.

As we'd been running, we could hear the rescue efforts. Men with Yorkshire accents, one saying my dad was a silly sod, one saying he couldn't reach him. He'd got his foot caught in the roots of a tree close to the bank – if anything he wasn't deep enough. He'd lost his balance and been sucked under by a powerful current. I found that out later, and it helped to know that he hadn't been a silly sod. But at the time, that comment, like the gash on my foot, didn't hurt and didn't matter. And then three young blokes tore off their shirts and waded in, shouting, 'Bugger this.' It seemed an odd thing to say when you're determined to save a man's life; like asking Death if he thinks he's hard enough to come outside and have a go. There was a bend in the river, so Mum and I had to turn inland and out of sight to get closer. By the time we reached my brother, they'd hauled Dad out and rolled him on his side. As if by some miracle – perhaps Fate felt guilty and decided to make amends – a woman pushed through the huddle and said she was a nurse. She knelt down and worked some magic on my dad's clogged lungs so that he spewed out a gobful of murky liquid. Then one of the shirtless men looked at me and said: 'Do you want to give him a kiss?' and Dad lifted his eyes towards us and gave a feeble, sheepish grin.

That hot summer day cast a long shadow. My dad recovered in what seemed like minutes. He was relieved, exhausted and grateful, but his prevailing emotion seemed to be embarrassment. I suppose that's understandable. He'd been nearly unconscious when they pulled him from the water, so his first clear memory was of vomiting in front of his wife, his children and an inexplicable audience of strangers. My mum, who had long before committed herself to a lifetime of expecting the worst possible outcome, carried henceforth the air of a woman vindicated. For her, this was not a story of how my father had been rescued, but of how even a harmless riverside picnic could prove to be the death of you. My brother, who had saved Dad's life by screaming for help, was nevertheless haunted by the fact that he'd been unable to pull him free all by himself.

And me? I was fine for the first week or so. But that first realisation of my parents' mortality and my own; of the randomness of fortune – good and bad; and that not only could my dad not protect me from the scary realities of life, he couldn't even protect himself, was to have a slow-release effect. In the short term, I became too terrified to let my parents out of my sight, in case the minute I turned my back, they'd have some other near-death encounter. In the long term, I was left with only one noticeable scar: I couldn't swim.

Right through school, I was ashamed of it. Mum and Dad tried getting me private lessons, but I was always too scared, too knowing about the dangers, and incapable of seeing the fun. I never swam a width, never went underwater except by accident, never ventured out of the shallow end. I imagined that if I could just get to the other side of childhood, my problems would be over. No more compulsory lessons; no more excuses and embarrassment. I hadn't thought about the fact that people don't just swim because they have to, they swim because they want to. So even as an adult, I would find myself by the side of a pool on some holiday somewhere, apologising for my inability to join in. Occasionally, I'd lower myself in gingerly, the way I'd been taught to at my first ever swimming lesson, just so that I could cool off and talk to my friends or boyfriend eye to eye, rather than peering down at them from the sunbed. But once in, I didn't know what to do. I'd try to look casual and comfortable, maybe lean against the edge and kick out a solitary leg, but it was all a bit pathetic. Going into a pool felt like regressing to childhood. I couldn't do anything for myself. I just had to watch the grown-ups and pretend I understood.

Then one morning, I was lying on a sunbed watching my friend Sioned swimming. She wasn't doing anything fiercely athletic, just that peculiarly female way of swimming with your head out of the water so your hair doesn't go frizzy, and moving her arms slowly out and in. I was slightly hungover from dinner the previous night, so I felt sleepy and relaxed, and I remember thinking, 'I could do that.' Nobody else was there, or I might not have had the nerve, but I dipped down into the shallow end and had a go at leaning forward. My feet left the bottom of the pool for the first time without armbands or someone with a whistle supporting me, and it felt OK. Then it felt scary, so I stopped. But I tried again, and this time I moved my arms a little, copying what Sioned was doing in the deep end. It worked. I moved – along, not downwards. I did a few jerky strokes, then stopped again, gripped on to the side and settled myself, and then gave it another go. I was doing it. I could swim. Just.

The problem with me is I avoid the things that scare me. The deep end scared me. Being too far from the edge scared me. Feeling under pressure scared me. So for years and years, this was swimming to me – a few hasty strokes in the shallow end of an empty pool, unobserved, unskilled, unjudged. I didn't want to get any better, because I knew that that would mean having lessons, going underwater, being out of my depth. If I couldn't swim, I wouldn't drown. It really was an appealing theory.

I had children, and one of the things I promised myself was that they would learn to swim. Grandma's thesis didn't apply to them. I wasn't going to put them at risk, and I wasn't going to let them share my humiliation. I took them paddling when they were babies, being careful not to instil my fear in them. But as soon as I could I signed them up for lessons, and it was after one of these – when their teacher was telling me how well they were doing, and I was feeling overwhelmed with pride and relief – that I let it slip that I couldn't swim. I think I expected her to gasp in horror, but she was pleasantly unsurprised. She told me she often taught adult beginners, and after a brief, incoherent monologue about how busy I was, and how I could kind of swim a bit anyway, just not in the deep end, and how I was better off not swimming really what with that hair-frizzing thing and everything ... I knew that I'd run out of excuses.

Before every lesson, I thought it must get easier. But it never did. I would drive to the pool in a state of anguish, and get changed in the sodden-floored dressing room as if it were a condemned cell. I hated the smell of chlorine, the way it stung my eyes as soon as I entered the building. I hated feeling cold *and* scared so that I didn't know where the shivering ended and the trembling began. I felt sick. I wanted to run away. It was the longest thirty minutes of my week.

OK. This is OK. Just treading water. I can see the side of the pool, I'm no more than a single panicky lunge away from it. This feels good. Could I kick my legs out and start swimming? No. Could I move further into the centre? No. Float on my back? Maybe next time. But for now, upright, bobbing a foot or two above the floor of the pool, making jerky, arrhythmic movements to keep me above the surface, aware of the anxiety like an undigested bolus in my gut, but keeping it from rising into my throat, for now this is OK. I allow the water to turn me slightly, so that I'm facing the shallow end. Three pre-school children are jumping gleefully into the water. I have never jumped into a swimming pool. I'm not sure I ever will. And yet, hearing their squeals and watching their ecstatic splashing, I try to comprehend the notion that this feeling – being out of one's depth – must be some people's idea of fun.

As if they'd never been

My grandmother had a sitting room that was kept for best. Nobody went in it, because it was there for 'visitors', and no one who came to the house ever quite merited that description. So for much of her life, she consigned herself to a small fraction of her living space and left the larger part unoccupied in case somebody one day popped in and judged her on it.

Like many of her generation, Grandma Dolly kept a tidy house. People of my age have learned to pass off a bit of mess as characterful. It's what happens when you lead busy lives. My grandmother's generation led busy lives too, of course, with umpteen children and jobs to hold down. And unlike us, they couldn't do their shopping online or drive to supermarkets. They'd walk to the shops to buy actual ingredients and cook actual meals, rather than warming up a plastic-wrapped slab of salt and hydrogenated fat to wolf down while watching a TV chef make bouillabaisse. Her generation didn't have washing machines or dishwashers, but they still managed to find the time to clean the front step, a part of the house that nobody born since 1960 – myself included – would ever consider worthy of a buffing up. If my grandmother's generation saw the mess we live in, they wouldn't consider it quirky, they'd consider it slatternly. Our standards have slipped, and I for one thank God for it.

But for Grandma Dolly, who'd grown up in whatever cramped, rented accommodation her immigrant parents could afford, owning a house was a massive deal, and looking after it, 'keeping it nice', was a central tenet of her existence.

Grandma was a tiny bundle of energy and determination. Even in old age, she kept her hair dyed brown and set in the same wave she'd worn since before the war. Her appearance was made the more arresting by her right eye, which was half hazel and half green. Once you'd noticed it, your own eye was inexorably drawn to look at it. She was only four-foot-ten and slight in build, but when in her eighties she was run over by a van and, according to a witness, 'thrown into the air like a rag-doll', she came out of it with barely a bruise. She was tough and uncompromising. If she liked you, she could be twinkly and funny, solicitous and sweet. Dare to cross her though and you would be consigned to the outer darkness for ever and a day. Given this unwillingness to tolerate people who annoyed her, she didn't go in much for socialising. Her husband died relatively young, when I was less than a year old. As a child, I imagined that Grandma's increasingly reclusive nature was the result of her grief at losing him; and in part it was. She certainly never got over his death. But as I got older, I realised there was more to it than that. She spent a lot of time at our house, and whenever we had visitors, Grandma would insist on helping us tidy up afterwards. Our house was always messy, my parents being early adopters of the notion that life's too short to spend it dusting, but in spite of their best efforts to stop her, she would diligently set to work the minute the guests had left, or sometimes, if my mother couldn't find a polite way of removing the dustpan from her grasp, while they were saying their goodbyes. When the final cushion was plumped, the last crumb hoovered up, Grandma would say with some pride: 'There. It's as if they'd never been.' And that, I began to realise, was the point. A tidy house was an end in itself. It didn't need to be shared with others to be enjoyed. And as the years of her long life gathered behind her, she appeared to have come to the conclusion that the best way to keep her home fit for others to see, was never to allow anyone in to see it.

Throughout my childhood, I only went to Grandma's house about a dozen times. If we popped in on our way home from the library or something, she'd be pleased to see us, but not over-eager for us to stay. We'd be invited in for a cup of tea, but the kitchen acted as a sort of holding pen; you could come so far into her domain, but no further. I remember asking to see into the living room, and she let me open the door and look, but there was no way we were going to go and sit in it. It fascinated me, not only because it was tacitly out of bounds, but because in its decor and furnishings it had remained utterly unchanged since the 1940s. Indeed many years after her death, I went with my children to a museum of interior design, and saw a room that was almost identical. The three-piece suite, the old table-sized radio in pride of place, the strange painted masks of Rita-Haythorthesque glamour girls adorning the walls, everything was just like Grandma's house. There was a rope in front of the room at the museum, stopping you from going in and sitting down, and that felt a bit like Grandma's house too.

But for all her desire to keep her house to herself, she nevertheless craved our company, and we loved hers. She came to us three times a week on average. She was the matriarch of the family, ever present and ever welcome. Following the too-early death of my other grandma when I was seven, Grandma Dolly became the first person you'd call when your exam results came in, or if you were made a prefect. If you had a new skirt, you could model it in front of her, knowing that she'd say, as she always did: 'I wish you well to wear it.' With new shoes it was: 'I wish you well to tear them,' both incantations from a time when being a child was no guarantee that you'd outlive your clothes, let alone your shoe leather.

She wasn't, it's fair to say, a cheery presence. Her natural view of life was that it was out to get you. I remember sitting with her one night and watching Fred Astaire on the *Parkinson* show. Fred, dapper and lithe at the age of eighty or so, tap-danced down the stairs to greet his host. My grandmother watched him through eyes narrowed by a combination of myopia and cynicism. 'How old is he?' she asked. 'Over eighty,' my dad replied. Grandma mumbled some dismissive Yiddish monosyllable and shook her head in despair. 'It's a bastard,' she said, glowering at this sprightly hoofer dancing in the face of death.

She was often unintentionally funny, not least because she was such an archetype of the Jewish mother – fiercely proud of our achievements, and pretty unimpressed by everyone else's, fearful, pessimistic and deeply superstitious. If we told her we were going on holiday, she'd say, 'You go. Enjoy. Don't worry about me.' And the subtext was, quite clearly, that it wouldn't kill us to picture her in solitary despair once in a while.

But she was also funny by design; she enjoyed puncturing pomposity with a shrug or an offhand comment, and this habit continued right up to the end of her life. The last time I saw her, she was in a hospital bed, morphine-medicated and apparently barely conscious. The family had gathered round the bedside, knowing there was very little time left to spend with her. As it happened it was my birthday, and I had just started dating a handsome young radio producer. In the gloom of the room, and unable to think of anything worthwhile to say to the comatose figure in front of us, my aunt asked me where my new man had taken me for my birthday. 'He treated me to tea at The Ritz,' I said, half-heartedly. 'Did you hear that, Mum?' asked my dad. No reply. 'He took her to The Ritz.' Grandma lay motionless, but her brow furrowed slightly, and on a weak, rasping out breath she whispered her one-word verdict on the man who, some years later, I would marry: 'Flash.'

On the day of her funeral, we gathered at her house to wait for the cortège. Sitting in the kitchen didn't seem to be an option, as it was too small for us all, and it felt wrong to be in there without Grandma pottering about reaching for the biscuit tin. So we sat in the front room instead, squashing the upholstery of the three-piece-suite for the first time in decades. We made small talk in lowered voices, not sure whether it was appropriate to smile or laugh, so sticking to platitudes and staring at our hands. The huge old radio dominated the room, and my dad, attempting to lighten the gloom, decided to see if it still worked. He fiddled with a few dials and a burst of static, white noise punctured the awkward silence. He carried on twiddling, and all at once the room was filled with the mellifluous voice of pre-war crooner Al Bowlly.

'Good night, sweetheart, till we meet tomorrow, Good night, sweetheart, sleep will banish sorrow.'

This room that my grandmother had taken such pains to preserve had transported us all back in time. Three generations of her family had gathered to sit in it, in clear defiance of convention. We had flattened the cushions and put teacups on the table. We had, merely by our presence, made it untidy. Fifty years had passed through Grandma's sitting room since the first time she'd got it the way she wanted it to look. She'd tried her hardest to keep it that way, and we, through grief at her passing, had come along and messed it all up. But with that one eerie blast of music, Bowlly and his dance band had been summoned by Grandma to plump up the cushions, sweep up the cake crumbs and tidy those fifty years away. It was, as she might have put it herself, as if they'd never been.

The end of the peer show

When Margaret Thatcher died, amid all the eulogising and demonising, a small curiosity began doing the rounds of the social networking sites. It was a video clip from an interview the Baroness had given, after her retirement from public office, to a Scandinavian broadcaster. The journalist conducting the interview, having come to the end of the serious stuff, was left with just the quirky, off-the-wall 'And finally ...' question, meant to lighten the mood and show a softer, more cuddly side to her subjects.

'All the people that I interview,' she began in her nearly flawless English, 'I ask them to do something for me.' And you could tell from the awkward, beseeching lean towards Mrs Thatcher that she knew this was going to be a long shot.

'It's a kind of gimmick on my show and it's ... to make a jump ... just to stand up and make a jump up in the air.'

Before she could elaborate any further on this concept, the Iron Lady was bringing down the shutter.

'I shouldn't dream of doing that,' she replied.

The interviewer gamely pressed on, laughing an increasingly

high-pitched, nervous laugh at every one of Mrs Thatcher's flat refusals, while admitting that they'd had a bet in the office beforehand and she'd told them this was never going to happen. The former prime minister was adamant, immoveable, true to her formidable reputation. She said it was silly, puerile. Why on earth would she do it?

'Gorbachev did it,' the journalist ventured. It was a brave attempt, but a stupid one. Mrs Thatcher gave her a withering look.

'You amaze me,' she said, bristling with schoolmistressy disapproval.

'I wonder what he thought of the politics of a free society if that's what they ask you to do.'

The interviewer gave it one last go, explaining that many people found it fun, a chance to show a different side of themselves.

'I'll tell you what it shows: it shows that you want to be thought to be normal or popular,' countered Mrs Thatcher. And that, unmistakeably, was that.

I think the reason so many people liked this little snippet was that it reinforced the lack of humour they had long suspected of their erstwhile leader. A jump, a little jump. What possible harm could it do? Some people really need to lighten up.

The problem for me watching it, as someone who resolutely disliked what Mrs Thatcher stood for, was that I couldn't help applauding what in this instance she *wouldn't* stand for, what she was never in a million years going to stand for – to leap around in an asinine manner on a chat show. The very intransigence that I'd always found so alarming, so mystifying, so unsympathetic, was in this instance something I could only respect. A jump is not a chance to show a different side to yourself; it's a chance for a TV producer to show that they've got one over on you. 'Even once-mighty people will jump when I tell them to,' the producer can declare, 'for I am Oz the great and powerful and nobody wants to look like a party pooper on camera.'

When my children were small, I spent a great deal of time and energy warning them about peer pressure. It seemed to me that the roots of many of life's problems lay here – in the desire to fit in. So I would diligently explain to them that nobody could make you do a dare, for instance, or try a cigarette or take drugs, and that being different wasn't the same as being unpopular. In my own childhood, I had seen how the need to fit in had made people do things they were uncomfortable about, even ashamed of. It seemed to me then, and it still does, that you could place most of the ills that afflict young people (bullying, gangs, the sexualisation of young girls to name just a few) squarely at the door of our pathetic desire to be accepted. So surely, if we could tackle that at its source, if one of the first things we taught our kids was not just to say 'no', but to say it forcefully and with a smile on their faces – 'no, that's a stupid idea, why on earth would anyone do that?' – then perhaps a whole lot of misery could be avoided.

But of course it's not that simple. Peer pressure is endemic in our culture. Take the Mexican wave, for example. Come on, indulge me a little. I know where I'm going with this. When my son was about seven, I took him to see his favourite band play at a huge arena. In the hiatus between the support group finishing and the main act arriving on stage, somebody on the other side of this cavernous space decided that we, the audience, should become one. We had to bond, we had to abandon our individuality, break down the invisible barriers between us, and become a cheering, stomping, amorphous, music-loving mass. One by one, then row by row, block by block, thousands of once-proud, inhibited, easily embarrassed English people leapt to their feet, arched their backs, threw up their arms in a near-orgasmic gesture of submission and shouted 'Whoa'. I saw it coming towards us with a threatening and unstoppable momentum, and so did my son.

'Oh cool,' he exclaimed.

'Oh shit,' I muttered.

'Can we join in?' he asked, delightedly.

'We'll probably have to,' I replied, grimly, and then not wanting to sound like a killjoy, I added unconvincingly, 'which is great.'

For me, the Mexican wave was a symbol of oppression, a metaphor for the mindless subservience of the herd, the very definition of a futile gesture. Here was my chance to make a point, to put the case for individuality. Right here, right now, I could teach my son that we all speak with our own voice; that even if the rest of your gang are racist or sexist or homophobic or smoking crack, it's OK to go against the tide, to sit down and be counted. You are not just part of a greater 'Them', you are and always will be 'You', my son.

He, however, was poised on the edge of his seat, desperate to join in with something greater than he had ever known. He wanted to be part of the machine, and worse, he badly wanted me to be too. The wave was, by now, hurtling towards us. What would I do?

I joined in. Of course I did. I'm not a total arse. It was, after all, a Mexican wave, not the Cultural Revolution. The only lesson my refusal would realistically have taught him was that his mother took herself too seriously. He was happy, I was momentarily embarrassed – neither of us lost our identity. But the Mexican wave was just the beginning. At the other side of the auditorium, the crowd had started doing the moves to 'YMCA'.

People will do the most ludicrous things if they think it'll be more embarrassing not to. Go up to one person in that audience on their own and ask them to leap to their feet and shout 'Whoa', and I guarantee they wouldn't do it. We don't mind being a bit 'crazy' as long as everybody else is being 'crazy', because then it doesn't seem ... well, crazy. In fact it would be crazier not to. A Mexican wave is as harmless as it is pointless, of course, but it is in its way a mass movement, and like all mass movements, to join in with it is an abdication of both responsibility and power. Because there are only two ways you can have power in this scenario – if you're the one who starts the movement or if you're the one who stops it. Most people, as Mrs Thatcher said, will join in in order to be thought 'normal and popular'.

Audience participation relies on just this sort of peer pressure, which is why I hate it so much. I've seen it from both sides: as a performer – demanding, expecting, relying on audience members to behave in a certain way – and as a punter desperately hoping not to be picked on. So I understand how the dynamic works. The performer is 99 per cent confident that whoever they select will do what they want them to do, just for the sake of a quiet life and not falling foul of the herd. But trust me, if you decide not to join in, you are the one with the power.

Now I admit, it sounds pathetic even to think of it in those terms, but when you sit in an audience, you very often don't want to be singled out. And yet when you are, it can feel like you have no choice but to go along with it. Picking on members of the audience – however amusingly and inventively done – is ultimately the recourse of someone short of ideas. I apologise to my comedian friends for saying that, especially since some of them are quite spectacularly good at this spontaneous interaction – and if the audience members involved are happy with that, then great. But the performers need you more than you need them, and if you refuse to join in, you expose this. It's a mean trick, sure, but then so is dragging some poor sucker up on stage and humiliating them.

I discovered this during a comedy show at the Edinburgh Festival. I'd just come off stage from my own show and was tired and hungry, so not in the most receptive of moods. But I'd heard great things about this particular comedian, so I thought I should try to catch him. A short while into his act, he announced that for the next section he was going to need a member of the audience. I desperately didn't want to be picked – after all, I'd done my performing for the night, going back on stage would have been something of a busman's holiday. So I lowered my head and tried to avoid eye contact as the comedian went from table to table weighing up his prey. Finally, of course, he picked on me.

'You'll do,' he said, and I knew I was supposed to give a weary look of resignation and follow him onto the stage. But I really didn't want to, so I smiled and shook my head.

'Come on, on your feet,' he said.

It seemed a *fait accompli*. The audience was already applauding me. And that, I realised, is what makes people do it: your whole peer group, relieved that it's you and not them, is willing you to obey orders, partly so that the show can go on, but also to make damn sure he doesn't change his mind and pick on them. I knew it would be easier to play along, but the more pressurised I felt, the less inclined I was to do it. I'd come to watch a show, not to be in one. With as charming a tone as I could muster, I said, 'No thanks. You'd better ask someone else.' But he wouldn't move on. It had become a power struggle between us. I hadn't sought it, but I certainly wasn't going to cave in.

He had one more tactic up his sleeve. My shoulder bag was strung over the back of my seat, and he suddenly grabbed it and ran up to the stage. He threw it towards the curtain at the back and then, returning to centre-stage, said triumphantly: 'That'll get her up here.'

It had an odd effect on the audience, some laughing and applauding, but others audibly gasping, tutting and siding with me. He was right, though. I had to go up on stage now. So I did. I walked past the comic, retrieved my bag and went to sit back down with it. But as I passed him he tried to get it off me again. We tussled in this undignified fashion for longer than we should have done. I think we'd sort of forgotten about the show; we were now just two strangers having a fight in public. Eventually, and without really knowing what I was doing, I whacked him hard on the arm with my bag. He looked genuinely stunned, let go of the strap and I walked back to my seat to a round of applause. It was a pyrrhic victory. I'd ended up part of the show after all, looking far more ridiculous than I would have done if I'd just played along. But his refusal to let me just sit and watch had become a kind of bullying, and my not giving way felt pathetically like a win.

The odd thing about this whole episode is that I'm someone who obeys rules. I don't have a rebellious nature. But I have to believe that the rules are there for a purpose, that they've been imposed by someone who broadly has my best interests at heart. To do something I'm told to do purely because it will make me look like an idiot offends even *my* eagerness to comply.

It's the Mexican wave problem all over again – a seemingly harmless bit of nonsense with faintly sinister overtones. I can't be the only who worries about these things, and it makes me wonder if we shouldn't all routinely refuse to do stuff that society tells us to do, just for the practice. I'm not suggesting we break laws; heaven forbid. Little acts of rebellion – wearing odd socks, red wine with fish, milky Earl Grey – might just be enough one day to save us from tyranny.

Take it too far though, and you risk cutting off your nose to spite your face. I could give you a long list of things I have refused to experience – plays I've deliberately missed, films I've eschewed, books I've spurned, and on and on – for no better reason than that everyone else was reading it, watching it, doing it, banging on about it, and I refused to bow to the pressure. It includes seeing *Les Misérables*, taking drugs, skiing, eating bacon sandwiches, buying a motorbike, having sex on a first date, reading *The Lord of the Rings*, listening to Van Morrison and squash (the game, not the fruit drink).

It was this very resistance to peer pressure that stopped

me getting my ears pierced as a teenager ... well, that and a faint suspicion that making holes in bits of flesh that didn't originally have them was a flawed idea. For years and years, I proudly flaunted my unmutilated lobes, preferring instead to suffer all day from the unique dragging pain caused by clip-ons. But then, when my daughter – as a result of peer pressure, I might point out – got her ears pierced without any fuss at all, I decided to give it a go. I was forty-five and it made me feel young again. It's a toss-up now what I'll try next – sex on a first date is tricky when you're married, but more appealing than reading *The Lord of the Rings*. Maybe I'll opt for squash.

Refusing to go with the majority for the sake of being different can be every bit as mindless as following with ovine conformity. Somewhere between Mrs Thatcher's refusal to be 'normal' and jumping off a cliff because your friends tell you to, there's probably a healthy attitude. In an ideal world, we would all take decisions for ourselves, based on the best available information, and without feeling the need either to join in or stand alone. This is not, alas, an ideal world.

I recently went for a walk in the country with my family. It had been unseasonably rainy, so the route was muddy and in places impassable. I was following along at the back of the group, whistling a little tune to myself in the manner of Winnie-the-Pooh, when we reached a swamp where there had previously been a field. My son weighed up the situation and decided on the best place for us to cross.

'It's not too deep here, but I'd do it fast if I were you,' he called over his shoulder, and bounded gazelle-like across the deep mud. Phil followed, perhaps more stag-like than gazelle, but still pretty impressive. Then my daughter, dancing across like a young Leslie Caron. I stopped and looked around me. I had a feeling this might not be the best place. It looked pretty deep to me, and we'd passed somewhere further back that seemed altogether more sensible. But they'd all done it and I didn't want to seem like a wuss. I stepped gingerly across, too slowly, allowing my weight to settle into the bog, contrary to my son's advice. By the time I reached the other side, my boots were squelching with a thick internal coating of mud and my trousers were soaked to the thigh.

We carried on a little further and this time had to cross a stream. I was quite some way behind by now, not least because I was carrying within my footwear copious quantities of turf, but since Phil and the kids were in the distance, I could please myself. I decided I wasn't going to succumb to peer pressure. I'd failed to follow my instincts first time around, and look where it had got me. I found a place where I would be comfortable crossing, and carefully picked my way across the stream, feeling the water seeping through into my mud-filled boots. True, my trousers got wet all over again, but I didn't fall in, and I felt pretty pleased with myself. I'd chosen an independent course and followed it.

I caught up with the others. My daughter turned round and looked at my sodden legs.

'What happened?' she asked.

It was then that I noticed her trousers were completely dry.

'There was a bridge just up to the right,' she explained.

'A bridge? Why didn't somebody tell me?'

'We just assumed you'd do what we were doing,' she said. 'You know, like a normal person would.'

And are there many vegan train drivers in France?

'And are there many vegan train drivers in France?'

Yet again, my mother was trying to navigate out of a conversational cul-de-sac. It happened at every social gathering. She'd end up in the corner of a room, stuck in a one-sided attempt at dialogue with the person everybody else, by some sixth sense, was avoiding. She doesn't like to give up on people, that's the trouble. It's something that she's instilled in us too, but as the years have gone by, I've often wished she'd also taught us how to extricate ourselves from small-talk hell.

The problem is that a lot of people are terrible at conversations, failing to understand the basic principle: I ask you a question, you ask me one in return. It's a pretty simple, transactional process. If what I get from you is something – a notion, a world view, information about your job or your pet or your personal life – that I recognise, something I can share with you, then a nice easy flow of story and counter-story can ensue. And if what I get from you is something that I've never come across before, even better. We can debate, learn, grow from the encounter.

That's what ought to happen. But it rarely does. More often than not it's like this: I ask you something, you give me a brief answer. I don't *hear* your brief answer because you've made no effort to raise your voice over the loud music and the gales of laughter from all those people having way more fun than we are. You don't ask me something in return. So now I have to come up with a supplementary question, which doesn't reveal the fact that I didn't actually catch your answer to my first one. You answer the second question with a little more detail and, thanks to my cupping my ear and craning in your direction, a little more volume.

If we're lucky, I've now cottoned on to what you do, or where you live, or how you know the host. If I haven't, we're in trouble, because there's no way you're coming back with a question for me. No sir. You're strictly a passenger on this particular journey; I'm going to be the one driving the car, reading the map and choosing the music.

There's a really simple phrase that would avoid all this anguish, if only everyone deployed it. 'And how about you?' That's it. Four little words that turn an interrogation into a chat.

'Have you come far?'

'No, just a couple of miles. And how about you?'

And we're off on a voyage of discovery with remarkably little effort.

I don't understand why people seem so reluctant to give it a go. In my professional life, I often have to do a whole day of press interviews, and after a while, I get so sick of the sound of my own voice, of hearing myself regurgitating the same stories again and again, that I'm crying out to use it. Sometimes I do, just to shake things up a bit. 'Do *you* have kids? Did *you* get caught in that rain this morning?' Something, anything, to acknowledge that even though I'm there promoting a programme, we're both human beings with something to say.

But maybe that's the point – most people, in their everyday lives, don't get asked to talk about themselves. So when someone shows an interest in them, they get a little giddy and the rules of social intercourse go clean out of their heads. Thus, people like my mother get deeper and deeper into the minutiae of what and where and why and how long and isn't that expensive and what qualifications do you need, until somebody, usually my father, mercifully interrupts to tell her it's time to go home.

My parents didn't go to a lot of parties when I was young. But when they did, Dad would complain for days in advance that he didn't want to go and wasn't going to enjoy himself. Mum, in spite of all previous experience would look forward to it. She'd plan her outfit, do her hair and anticipate a modestly glittering evening of fun and chat. But on their return, it was always the same story: Dad had talked to 'an amazing guy who puts out industrial fires' or 'this brilliant woman who was trying to develop a vaccine for malaria' or 'an incredible couple who've just sold their house to become crofters on the Isle of Arran'. Mum, meanwhile, had got stuck in the kitchen with 'someone in logistics' who, even under relentless questioning, had failed to reveal anything other than that the hours weren't too bad and he and his wife were thinking maybe Norfolk again this year.

And now here she was trapped again, with a vegan Parisian

train driver refusing to give her more than a surly monosyllable in return for her interest in him. But this time, we were all there listening, and Dad decided she'd tried hard enough and it was about time someone helped her out a bit.

'We love France,' he said with his most charming smile. 'We love French food, don't we, Sheila?'

Mum nodded and did a sort of lip-smacking gesture. The train driver looked at the carpet.

'Especially the bread,' my dad continued. 'Am I right, Sheila?'

'Oh yes. Croissants. Wonderful.'

'And baguettes. Freshly baked.'

Still, he gave them nothing.

'So crusty.'

Rien.

'You don't need anything on it. Not even butter.'

My brother and I watched, fascinated by how anyone could withstand this joint charm offensive, but still the train driver did nothing more than pick a little dirt from his fingernail. Dad was getting desperate.

'I mean, I'd love to know how they make it so delicious. What do they put in it? To make it so ... you know ... irresistible?'

The train driver looked my father in the eye for the first time, then curled his lip in barely concealed disgust and replied, 'Poison.'

There aren't many vegan train drivers in France, just as there weren't many vegetarian guesthouses in Scotland back in 1977. But there was at least one, and we – with an unerring instinct for the bizarre – had elected to stay there.

Being vegetarian used to be considered pretty odd. There were some urban vegetarians, ex-hippies, still hanging on to their principles in tall, old houses with scrubbed pine doors. But we weren't like them. We were Jews for a start; not even cool, kibbutznik Jews, but suburban Jews. We 'kept kosher', and lived among endless rows of 1930s semis with other suburban Jews also 'keeping kosher', while sneaking the odd bit of bacon if the rabbi wasn't looking. We ate what they ate (apart from the bacon – my parents were either too observant or too superstitious for that). We had chicken soup on Friday nights and chopped liver on Sundays. We followed the dietary laws of Leviticus and North-East London.

Dad was the first one in the family to turn. I have a faint memory of him telling me that it was walking past an abattoir on his way to work that finally put him off. But many years later, recalling that he'd worked at the time in an advertising agency in Mayfair, I began to wonder if I'd got the wrong end of that story. And besides, Jewish or not, he'd just art directed a campaign for British Pork, so clearly these scruples sneaked up on him unexpectedly. But one day he decided he'd had all the wurst and salt beef he could take for one lifetime. From now on he was going to be a friend to the Animal. Mum elected to join him. Perhaps she too was sickened by the slaughter of innocent lambs among the luxury car showrooms of W1. But more likely it was just simpler not to have to make two dinners.

From this epiphany onwards, my parents led a double life, cultivating yoghurt and sprouting mung beans in the airing cupboard while picking the smoked salmon off bagels at weddings and bar mitzvahs. My brother and I only ate meat when Grandma Ivy cooked it for us, but after she died we were happy to go without, and somehow never really missed it.

It wasn't just the four of us. At some earlier time, and for reasons that I never discovered, my mother's aunt Rachel and her husband had gone veggie too. Which is where the Scottish guesthouse comes in.

Aunt Rachel was a morally upright, somewhat formidable maths teacher. She was kind and loving but in a distinctly low-key way, so as children we found her intimidating. She adored my mother (though I'm sure the word 'adored' was too gushy for her lexicon) and the two of them grew even closer after Grandma Ivy died. Rachel and her more approachable husband Frank were what seemed to me hard-core vegetarians. They drank grape juice, while my parents let us have cherry-ade. They prepared nut roasts and lentil rissoles, while we had the food everyone else was eating as a side dish – cauliflower cheese or jacket potatoes – and simply missed the meat bit out. And whereas we would go to normal hotels and restaurants, and just put up with the lack of suitable food, Rachel and Frank became aficionados of the vegetarian hospitality trade.

One summer, they generously treated us to a few days in one of these establishments – a Bates-motel lookalike in the Lake District. It was silent but for the unwelcome footfall of guests crushing the carpet-pile. There was a gong that struck for supper, tolling in the catering with pretty accurate foreboding. And just in case you were thinking of letting your hair down a bit, it was dry. Mum and Dad have never been big drinkers, but nothing makes you crave alcohol like being told you can't have it. And since this wasn't something my mother felt she could share with her aunt, we fell into a curious ritual. Each night of our stay, we would say goodnight early to Rachel and Frank, go up to our room and wait for maybe half an hour until we thought they'd be in bed. Then we'd sneak out, get past the front room window unseen by dint of a sort of Groucho Marx lope, and go to the hotel next door so Mum and Dad could have a snifter. Even at the age of eight, this struck me as a faintly ridiculous way to behave.

You would think then that when, some years later, we were discussing our forthcoming trip to Scotland, and Rachel and Frank recommended another vegetarian guest house, Mum and Dad would have done anything to avoid the same joyless experience. But no. They went ahead and booked it. Perhaps, mindful of the difficulties we'd had in Belgium, where my dad had been brought a plate of spinach with a side order of spinach, they wanted to ensure we stood a chance of eating some protein. But whatever the reason, here we were in another temple to asceticism.

The hotel was an austere converted manse in a lowland glen – all imposing stone and velveteen drapes. The interior design spoke more of hospitals than hospitality: the bedrooms clinical and over-bright, the bathrooms smelling of Dettol. There was nothing actually wrong with it, nothing you could complain about – it was just the last place on earth you'd want to have a holiday.

But it was when we walked into the dining room that we realised we were in for a challenging evening. The landlady, a graduate of the Mrs Danvers Charm School, greeted us, standing in front of one long table. 'We all eat together here,' she declared as if being forced to sit shovelling food with strangers was somehow a good thing. 'We like to encourage communality.' Dad gave a forced smile, while Mum said, 'Oh that sounds lovely,' in exactly the same tone as if she'd said, 'God, that sounds hideous,' since that was what she was thinking.

We settled ourselves at one end of the empty table, hoping that nobody else would come and we might get to eat as a family. After all, how many vegetarians were there likely to be in this part of Scotland? For a few moments we made small talk with each other in those awkward hushed voices that hotel dining rooms seem to call for.

'Looks like rain tomorrow.'

'That was quite a drive.'

'Something smells tasty.'

It was as if we'd instantly forgotten how to have a conversation even between the four of us. So much for communality. And then we heard the tense whispering of incomers.

'Tuck your t-shirt in, Andrew. Why did you wear your plimsolls?'

There at the door was a boy of about twelve, the same age as me. He stopped dead as he clocked the single table, and realised with horror that he might have to sit near a girl. Behind him was his mum, thin-faced and instantly blushing.

'Ooh, hello, goodness, one table. Do we all? Goodness. That'll be ... how lovely! Hello. Hello. I'm Helen.'

My parents introduced us all and Helen introduced Andrew.

'Now, Andrew, show them your t-shirt. Look at Andrew's t-shirt. You'll enjoy this,' she said, and she sounded so sure that we prepared our faces for the fun that unquestionably lay ahead.

Andrew's t-shirt bore a quirky, somewhat phallic cartoon of the Loch Ness monster and the legend 'I'm a haggis hunter'.

'I'm a haggis hunter,' Helen exclaimed. 'We just loved that, didn't we, Andrew? Being vegetarians. And Scottish. We thought that was a hoot. I'm a haggis hunter. Isn't that wonderful?' And she laughed a terrifying laugh. You know the sound that a tap makes when the water supply has been switched off for some time – rasping, gurgling and finally gushing forth in uncontrollable flow? Well, that was the sound Helen made. It was a laugh that signalled the end of a long drought of mirth.

We all laughed too, not because it was 'a hoot', but because it would have been cruel not to, and Helen and her mortified child took their places at the far end of the table.

After a few more moments of uncomfortable small talk, fresh voices were heard, and a man and woman in their fifties walked in, gave the same involuntary double take towards the seating arrangements and settled themselves reluctantly among us. They were Ian and Sue, we established, and all the adults had a brief but edifying chat about where we'd driven from and how long it had taken, what with the roadworks, until suddenly Helen piped up again.

'Andrew, show Ian and Sue your t-shirt. Look at Andrew's t-shirt, Sue. You'll enjoy this, Ian,' she said in a tone which suggested she'd instantly got the measure of their sense of humour and knew this would just about make their night.

Andrew wearily stuck out his chest, Ian and Sue gamely laughed at the t-shirt, Helen did her terrifying bray, my parents pretended to find it hilarious all over again, and my brother and I decided that communality was, frankly, a pile of crap.

And then Pierre arrived. He walked into the dining room alone and, unlike the rest of us, seemed unfazed by the prospect of a communal table, perhaps because he had no intention of talking to anyone. We all introduced ourselves again, and he made as little eye contact as he could get away with and sat down, smoothing his napkin on his lap and settling himself in for a quiet evening staring at it.

It was our hostess who told us his name was Pierre. Just about all the information we gleaned about him came from her – the fact that he was French and vegan and travelling alone. We assumed this was because he couldn't speak much English, and were inclined to be impressed by this lonely, frail-looking creature of mystery making his way in a foreign land without language skills or predictable eating habits. But then the landlady forced him into a few exchanges, and it quickly became apparent that he could speak English perfectly well, but frankly couldn't be arsed.

The food was brought in, and it was dismal. People who are vegetarian today have no idea what a dispiriting experience eating out used to be. It was grim in a mainstream restaurant, because there was nothing to eat, and it was often grim in a vegetarian restaurant too because what passed for cuisine was in fact sustenance. Nowadays, thanks to Indian, Italian and Lebanese restaurants where you can eat fabulous meals that just happen not to contain meat, it's a breeze to be vegetarian.

Not only that, but there are substitutes for meat these days. Now admittedly, these aren't really substitutes at all. They're just experiments in texture which let you create, say, the ghost of a shepherd's pie. But I often suspect the main reason the meat substitute was invented was to give anti-vegetarians something to sneer at.

I don't have a problem with people who think vegetarianism is pointless. And I have a certain sympathy for the more informed arguments I've encountered, about the place that cattle-farming holds in preserving the British landscape, for example. But almost none of the negative comments you get about being veggie – and God knows why so many people feel it's any of their damn business – are about the societal impact of animal husbandry. No, they're always about meat-free sausages. 'What did you give up meat for if you're just going to eat vegetarian sausages?' they say as if we're all idiots for not having thought this through. So let me attempt to explain: if I'd given up meat purely because it *looked* like meat, and then replaced it with stuff that still looked like meat, but didn't taste as good, then yes you'd have a reason to sneer – though it'd still be none of your business. But I don't abstain because the appearance of a sausage offends me; I happen to think sausages look bloody delicious. I just don't feel comfortable killing a pig to have one. And if someone could invent a steak that looks as good as the ones my husband cooks (firm, chewy, but meltingly soft) and that didn't need to be ripped out of a cow's guts, I'd be first in the queue. But they haven't, so I'm stuck with Quorn. Pity, don't mock. Or better still, shut up and do neither.

Anyway, having grown up in the Seventies, anything that means I never have to eat another cashew roast is a godsend.

'Cashew roast,' said my father as our hostess wheeled in the trolley, 'what a treat.'

We were all given a slab solid enough to carve your epitaph on, and invited to help ourselves to the boiled-to-buggery cauliflower and carrots. We sampled it, lied about how lovely it was and began joylessly to work our way through it.

'And where are you from, Pierre?' my mother asked, to lighten the mood.

Pierre put another forkful into his mouth, showing no apparent sign of having heard her. He looked out of the window, chewed for a bit, then just as he sensed someone might repeat the question, he slowly turned his head towards her, swallowed and replied, 'Paris.'

Everyone agreed Paris was very exciting, a wonderful city, and must be a marvellous place to live. Pierre gave a snort and a Gallic shrug, and took another mouthful of stodge.

'And what do you do, Pierre?' she continued, unable to countenance defeat.

Another forkful – he was virtually concave, you had to wonder where he was putting it all – further chewing, and another long look out of the window. My brother suppressed a giggle and Dad glared at him. Finally, after what seemed an age, Pierre said, 'I drive trains.'

All eyes turned to my mother. It was like a high-level game of tennis in which Pierre had just served a probable ace. Surely there was no way she could come back with anything. There were questions we all wanted answers to: how did he survive as a vegan in France, possibly the least vegetarian-friendly place on earth; and what the hell did his fellow train drivers make of this surly, cadaverous oddball. But these were not Mum's style, and after an anxious wait, she finally returned the serve:

'Long-distance, or just from ... stop to stop?' The ball hit the net.

There was a silence, broken only by the sound of Pierre shovelling mounds of cashew roast into his skeletal frame. The grown-ups tried to fill the void with little noises of delight at what a great evening this was turning out to be, when suddenly Helen remembered something she'd failed to do.

'Andrew, show Pierre your t-shirt. Pierre, you'll love this. Look at Andrew's t-shirt.'

Pierre chewed and gazed out of the window.

'Pierre. You must take a look,' she gamely continued, after all, it had been such a hit with everyone else. Then a thought struck her and she tried a different tack: 'S'il vous plaît. Regardez le ... t-shirt ... de Andrew.' Pierre did his slow, pained look round and fixed his gaze on Andrew's chest.

'Il dit "I am a haggis hunter". Je suis un ... do you know what haggis is? It's a Scottish ... savoury pudding.'

'Boudin?' offered my mum.

'Boudin, yes,' gasped Helen. 'Boudin de ... bits of sheep. It just struck us as the funniest thing, you know. Not the boudin. That's disgusting. But the t-shirt. Being Scottish and vegetarian. C'est très amusant, n'est-ce pas?'

None of us could bear the discomfort – Helen so desperately needed approval and Pierre so clearly had no intention of giving it. Damn his taciturnity, his lack of social graces, his refusal to pretend to enjoy something he clearly didn't. He was behaving the way we all wanted to behave and we hated him for it.

Mum and Dad reminded Helen how funny they thought the t-shirt was, but it wasn't enough for her; she was like a big game hunter who'd set her sights on a lion, and wasn't going to settle for a couple of aardvarks. Finally, a small sliver of humanity seemed to pierce Pierre's consciousness. He looked Andrew in the eye, and as if the word were being surgically removed from him, unsmilingly murmured, 'Funny.'

There wasn't a person in that room who hadn't now decided that communality was a terrible idea. All that was needed was for someone to be honest enough to say so, and we could have called it a night and gone up to bed. But no. Ian had an inspiration.

'Guess what I do for a living.'

'Ian ...' protested Sue.

'No, I think it'll be fun. See if they can guess.'

'Ian ...' she said again, with even more weariness in her voice, and I wondered if he made a habit of this.

Mum, still seeing it as her duty to keep the conversation going, jumped at this last-ditch attempt to salvage it.

'Ooh,' she said in a voice that suggested she couldn't remember when she'd been more excited. And since we'd been sitting there for an hour by now, it's quite possible that she couldn't.

'Well, it must be something unusual ... erm ... astronaut?'

There was a ripple of laughter, and Ian shook his head, grateful that someone was playing along.

'Pilot?'

'No. Keep trying.'

Sue rolled her eyes.

My dad decided to join in.

'Architect?'

'Doctor?'

'Vegan train driver?' my brother whispered, and got the look from Dad again.

'Bank manager?' proffered Mum.

'Pharmacist?' said Dad.

Things were hotting up now; Ian was right, this was fun ... or the closest we'd come to it since we'd entered this godforsaken hole.

A newly emboldened Helen offered up 'Haggis hunter' and we genuinely laughed this time.

'Racing driver?' I suggested.

'Football manager?' said Jeremy.

'Detective? Murder squad?' said my dad.

'Spy?' countered Mum.

'Baker!' shouted Sue in sudden exasperation. 'He's a baker. He's just a baker.'

There was a hideous pause. Then Ian said in a small, crushed whimper, 'I wanted them to guess.' And added somewhat redundantly, 'Anyway, I'm a *master* baker.'

A quarter of a century on from that night, and on a late winter's afternoon, Phil, the children and I had just completed a long country walk. We were cold and hungry and what we fancied more than anything was a proper cream tea. Phil remembered seeing a sign for one just a short distance from where we'd parked, so we used up our last resources of energy to find it. It was open; an ancient stone farmhouse with smoke spooling from its chimney.

We rang the bell and an amiable farmer came to the door. He showed us into the cosy beamed kitchen where tea was being served. There was just one long communal table.

'Take a seat,' he said, 'Anywhere you like. We just have the one table. We find it gets people chatting ...'

I looked at the table, at the roaring fire, at the trolley groaning with delicious-looking cakes, at my children's faces. And I thought of my mother: of her desperation to keep a conversation going; her genuine interest in people; her inability to get away from them; and of the fact that she'd passed all that on to me.

'You tuck in,' I said. 'I might just wait in the car ...'

Don't fence me in

'Welcome aboard this service from London Kings Cross to York. We hope you have a pleasant journey.'

'Oh sure,' I think, 'it's going to be just peachy.' The elderly man to my left settles into his seat and sneakily crooks his elbow across our shared armrest making a land-grab of my space. I let him get away with it since it matters so much to him, and anyway I have other things on my mind. I close my eyes and take a deep breath, but his jacket smells stale and now my lungs are full of someone else's sweat. I open my eyes again and look around. There's a couple across the aisle laughing helplessly and pouring themselves beer from a carrier bag full of cans. The little girl behind me sings a merry tune of her own composition, which is cute right now, but will quickly begin to pall. Now my neighbour, having invaded my seat space is pursuing *Lebensraum* on the table too. He's smoothed out his crossword right in the middle, and is tapping his pencil against my side of it for inspiration. 'Let the train take the strain,' was the slogan they used to use. I allow myself a grim smile and try to stop digging my fingernails into my leg.

The train plunges into a tunnel and I begin to count. One, two, three, four … it's a futile attempt to gain control. If I'm prepared, if I know for example that heading out of Kings Cross there are four twelve-seconders one after the other, or that just outside Grantham there's a twenty-seconder, then maybe I can relax in the knowledge that it won't take long before we're out in the daylight again. But it doesn't work. All that happens is that the tunnels become the focus of my journey, the only things I can think about. To a claustrophobic, a train in a tunnel is much the same as a lift in a lift shaft – an already enclosed space going inside another, darker, more oppressive one. I sit in my carriage looking out at fields, and the train feels spacious and airy. I look out at a tunnel wall and the same space shrinks around me. I'm shut in, and worse, I can only come out under someone else's guidance. If the train slows or stops, there is nothing I can do about it. I might as well be stuck in a lift, which to me is the same as saying I might as well be buried alive.

I know all this is illogical – I'm not an idiot. I know the train will emerge eventually; that even if it broke down, we'd all be walked along the tracks to freedom. But that doesn't make much difference, because the real place I'm trapped in is not the walls of the tunnel or the shell of the train; no, the real place I'm trapped in is my head. I'm not scared of going into a tunnel; I'm scared of going into a panic.

If you've never had a panic attack, then let me be the first to congratulate you. You've managed, thus far at least, to avoid quite one of the most unpleasant experiences it's possible to have while still, to the rest of the world, appearing to be doing nothing at all.

Imagine you're scuba diving. I never have, of course – way too risky – but there you are, having a lovely time of it with the coral and the fish and … oh look, I don't know. Like I said, I've never done it. Anyway, suddenly you come up to the surface and, just like the couple in that film *Open Water* (which I've never watched, of course – I have too much adrenaline rushing around in me as it is without sitting through something like that), you realise that the boat that was due to take you back to land has disappeared. You're completely alone in an endless sea. And that's when you spot the shark.

That utter terror and helplessness, that 'what the hell am I going to do now?' feeling, that bargain with yourself that if you ever get out of this alive you will never, ever do anything as stupid as scuba diving again? That's what a panic attack feels like. Only for me, it's not caused by a shark, but by a lift or a tunnel; for someone else it'll happen at a party, or looking down from a tall building, or simply walking down the street.

In case the scuba-diving analogy isn't working for you, I'll try to describe the symptoms: hot flushes, cold shivers, a racing pulse, the inability to breathe, the feeling that you want to run but you can't move a muscle, nausea, dizziness … that'll do for starters. And it all comes over you in a wave in a matter of seconds, sometimes completely out of the blue.

When I get panic attacks, they're usually connected with something that I know might bring them on – being in an enclosed space, or having some worry about my health … that sort of thing. For some unfortunate people, they come with no apparent cause at all. And here's the thing: once you've had one, the feeling is so overwhelmingly grim that you'll go to almost any lengths never to have one again. You start to avoid doing whatever you think might have triggered it. You become scared, not of the thing itself, but of the feeling it induced in you. You're frightened of being frightened. Anxiety is like one of those Escher drawings of a bafflingly endless staircase: it goes round and round on itself, with no obvious way of getting off.

There are all sorts of different therapies available, of course, and most of them will do the trick to some degree if you're open to trying them. But the catch-22 with all of them is this: the only way to cure a phobia is through exposure to the thing you're afraid of, and being exposed to the thing you're afraid of is very frightening, on account of you having a phobia about it. Thus, therapy is only as effective as you're brave enough to allow it to be.

In my case, cognitive behavioural therapy was successful at getting me to do long-haul flights because I wanted to go away with my family more than I wanted to avoid flying. But it didn't get me to start using lifts, because I would rather walk up twenty flights of stairs than spend five seconds inside a sealed metal box.

So the average anxiety sufferer can function quite normally for much of the time simply by not doing the things they're afraid of. But eventually, circumstances will dictate that you just have to. Then what do you do? The only thing that seems to work for me is total immersion in some other activity, which is of course easier said than done. It's hard to read a book or do a crossword, for instance, when your subconscious is yelling 'run like mad, we're all going to die'.

Some years ago, while filming a TV series, I opened a script to find a sequence where my character has a panic attack on a train. The writers were oblivious to the fact that I do in fact frequently have panic attacks on trains ... well, not all that frequently, but only because I avoid going on trains in the first place. I spent the entire night before filming having panic attacks about going on a train to play a woman who goes on a train and has a panic attack.

Contrary to what you might think, the best way to *play* having a panic attack is not actually to have a panic attack. Quite the reverse, in fact. When you're acting, you have to remember your lines and listen to the other actors and take notes from the director and think about which shoulder you had your bag on when you left the carriage in the previous scene and so on and so on. To do my job properly, therefore, I had to try to stay calm so that all the important stuff wouldn't go clean out of the (sealed-up, only open in case of emergency, designed to make you feel claustrophobic) train window.

Oddly, I needn't have worried. I had so much else to think about, I couldn't possibly find the time to panic. What appeared in the programme was a performance, an evocation of panic, not the real thing. Nobody knew, until we pulled into the station at the end of the filming day and I let slip a slightly hysterical sigh of relief, that I had any problem with trains at all, I'm glad to say. I thought that maybe I was cured; that facing my demons that day had seen them off for good. But the next time I went on a train, there it was again, the racing pulse, the fear in the pit of my stomach, the sickness. So I had two choices – either I had to have a film crew in tow every time I travelled by rail, or I had to get rid of my claustrophobia once and for all.

Ah, if only it were that simple.

One of the most infuriating things about anxiety is that the causes of it are entirely in your imagination. That's *not* the same as saying that it's your fault, you're putting it on, and you should just snap out of it; so let's put that idea to bed straight away. But being anxious is a habitual way of thinking that's devilishly easy to slip into and devilishly hard to shake off.

Suffering from anxiety doesn't just mean being a worrier, although worry is a part of it. The fatal combination, it seems to me – and I'm no expert on this, so forgive me if I'm talking out of my hat – is being a worrier and also having a tendency to 'catastrophise'. Catastrophising, as the name suggests, means leaping to the worst possible conclusion. Lots of people may worry when they get on a plane that it will crash. It'll cross their minds briefly, and then they'll settle down with the in-flight magazine and wonder what they ever did without a set of crystal-encrusted aeroplane cufflinks. If you're prone to catastrophising, however, you don't just *worry* that the plane will crash, you absolutely and beyond a shadow of doubt *know* it will. There's no point in buying crystal-encrusted aeroplane cufflinks because you'll never get the chance to wear them. Come to think it, though, there's also no point in *not* buying them. You won't be needing money where you're going. You might as well get them (and maybe a bottle of gin and a giant Toblerone) and then get back to preparing to meet your doom.

So the worries spark off the catastrophising, and the two together manage to turn a minor concern into a major fear. The more fearful you become about something, the more you will try to avoid it. But the more you avoid it, the more terrifying it becomes. And that – in my experience at any rate – is the root of anxiety. I worry, I become convinced I'm right to worry, I avoid whatever it is I'm worrying about and when I finally *do* have to face it, I panic.

There may be a predisposition to be this way. I come from a long line of worried women. The sort of women who never go to the cinema alone in case a dirty old man gropes them; who, every time the lights go down at the theatre, think they must be going blind; who hover uncomfortably above toilet seats for fear of coming into contact with someone else's microbes; who rarely lock lavatory doors without double checking the bolt won't stick and sometimes, in cases of particularly suspect hygiene, flush the chain with their feet. Oh yes, they are agile, these women, both in body and mind. They are the ninjas of worry, able to seek out causes of anxiety in the most innocuous of places. They have an unrivalled capacity to seize on snippets of ill-informed scaremongering and allow them to change their behaviour. Through the years, thanks to 'something I heard on the radio' or 'this article in the paper', they've worried about the health risks of burnt toast, white bread, honey, beansprouts, too much alcohol, too little alcohol, too much sunlight, too little sunlight, pollution, hair dye, metal fillings, green-tinged potatoes, tampons and pierced-earrings. Being wary, vigilant, constantly looking out for the little thing that could kill you, is a tough job, a full-time commitment, but someone's got to do it, and the women in my family are up for the challenge.

Worry is by no means the sole preserve of women. I know many men who are spectacularly good at it. It just happens that in my family it seems to be 'inherited' through the female line. But that may be changing. One day when my daughter was small she was playing a game of jumping from the table onto the sofa and back. I was watching her with a cup of tea, thinking I was being a pretty relaxed, fun kind of mum. But the combination of hard surfaces, jumping and hot drink were clearly bothering me more than I was aware. At one point, when I felt a little cautionary reminder might be in order, my daughter turned to me and said, with the weary air of one who'd heard nothing but warnings all morning, 'I *am* be-carefulling, mummy.'

It turned out that I hadn't been sitting quietly sipping my tea with an indulgent smile on my face at all. I'd been worrying. And worse, I'd been worrying out loud: 'Mind you don't fall, mind the hot tea, watch the wall, watch that corner, be careful, be careful, be careful.'

The fact that my daughter, at the age of five, had called me to account on it gave me some hope that maybe, just maybe, she wasn't going to be quite as anxious as her mother. Maybe she would break the mould.

The pernicious thing about anxiety is that it's often rooted in common sense. Jumping off a sofa onto a coffee table isn't a safe activity – if it were, let's face it we'd all be doing it. There are risks attached, and that's partly what makes it fun. Your job as a parent is to minimise those risks as best you can – not putting the hot cup of tea on the table between sips would be a start – and give a brief, clear set of guidelines, like 'try not to jump towards that sharp corner'. Continually saying 'be careful' means nothing, spreads the sense of anxiety to the child in a nebulous, confusing and unhelpful way, and devalues the phrase when there's really something to warn her about.

So maybe a part of my history of anxiety is that element of learned behaviour. But really that's just the beginning. What's made me the 'can't do' person I am today is a long-established pattern of avoidance. I cannot begin to express how full of admiration I am for people who continually challenge their fears and phobias. I face mine only as a matter of last resort.

It all started with Durham Cathedral. I was seven, and my parents had taken us there for an educational outing: a bit of brass-rubbing, the promise of a pencil-and-rubber set from the gift shop – this was what passed for fun in the 1970s.

We decided to climb the tower to enjoy the view. It was a beautiful summer's day, and unfortunately for me hundreds of other people had the same idea. Midway up the winding stair-case, something up ahead of us – perhaps an untied shoelace or a carelessly dropped Durham Cathedral keyring – caused someone to stop. At the same time there was a surge of people coming down, which meant that we found ourselves suddenly squashed in against an ancient stone wall, with people ahead of us, behind us and to the side of us. No one could move. There was a bit of jostling and everyone was starting to get cross.

I tugged my mum's sleeve and told her I didn't like it.

'Nobody likes it, darling, but we'll be at the top soon.'

'I don't want to go to the top. I just want to get out,' I said.

We looked behind us, but there was just a sea of heads and angry faces. There was no way out, not yet.

I *really* didn't like it now. I felt powerless and afraid, and for the first time I experienced the wave of feelings that I now understand to be panic. Eventually, the line of people ahead of us began slowly to shuffle forward, and we carried on to the top of the tower. We stood there looking at the view, taking big gulps of cool air, and I told my mum I wouldn't go back down that staircase for all the illustrated bookmarks in the gift shop.

'You have to, Bec. It's the only way down.'

'Well, I can't do it,' I said.

Nobody answered me at first, though I distinctly remember hearing Mum whisper to Dad, 'What do we do then? We can't bloody well throw her off.'

I did go down, of course, with my eyes half shut and my hand firmly gripping my mum's. But I'd made up my mind that I would never go up a church tower again.

Now that in itself wouldn't have been much of a problem. There isn't a glut of medieval spiral staircases in suburban Essex. Two weeks later, though, Mum and I were on a crowded tube train. I'd just been fitted for a particularly hideous bridesmaid's dress, I remember, so it hadn't been the best of days. The train stopped in a tunnel, as it often did, just outside Liverpool Street station. We waited and waited. People began sighing and swearing under their breath, and suddenly I was aware of the same feelings I'd felt in the tower of Durham Cathedral. I had to get out of there now. And I knew there was no way I could.

So now it was church towers and tube trains. Later it would be *all* train tunnels, then, at different times, road tunnels, basements, windowless rooms, lifts and on and on and on. Each time something made me feel uncomfortable, I vowed never to experience it again. It's a pattern I've carried on sporadically all through my life – see other chapters in this book, on swimming and school. Every now and then I make a concerted effort to deal with it: I start using trains again or learn to swim or fly long haul. But it seems as soon as I quash one fear, then another pops up somewhere else.

My saving grace is that I'm a pragmatist: when I really need to do a thing, I can do it – especially where my family or my work are concerned. I didn't use tube trains for years, until I went to drama school on the other side of London. Once I realised that it would take me three times longer to get in in the mornings by bus, miraculously I wasn't afraid of the tube any more. Within a year of leaving drama school, after another lengthy delay in a tunnel, I was back being terrified of them again. But when my first professional acting job meant travelling round Europe, I managed to conquer my fear of flying. The fact that these phobias come and go – though they're no less powerful when they're there – does at least make me realise that it's possible to deal with them even if only for a while. But since that first panic attack in Durham Cathedral tower, I don't remember a time when I didn't have a phobia at all. Anxiety in some form is always with me. It slightly shocks me to think of it, but I've been afraid longer than I've been married, longer than I've been a mother, longer than I've been an actress. Fear is a significant part of who I am.

Phil is fond of quoting a phrase from Hilaire Belloc. In the Cautionary Tale 'Jim', a little boy runs away from his scary nanny only to get eaten by a lion. The moral of this story is 'always keep a hold of nurse for fear of finding something worse'. Phil's theory, and it's a good one, I think, is that I can cope with the nerve-wracking things particular to my life

– the things that would induce anxiety in other people – by clinging on to these little pockets of avoidable fear. I can, for example, take part in a debate with the prime minister, or be the only woman on a panel-game, or perform on live TV, and be relatively relaxed about it. I just can't take the train home afterwards. A phobia, by this definition, is a way of controlling fear. The trouble is that when I have to do the thing I've been avoiding, the fear starts controlling me.

The train comes out of the tunnel. I can breathe again. I try to relax my shoulders a little; to stop sitting bolt upright, peering ahead through the windows of the carriage, trying to guess when we'll next disappear into the gloom.

Under my breath, I start to whistle a little tune to cheer myself up. It's an old Bing Crosby number. Where did that suddenly come from?

'Just give me land, lots of land under starry skies above. Don't fence me in.'

The elderly gentleman gives me a sidelong glance, and lets me have the armrest back.

Rainy days and Mondays

At the age of eleven, I decided I had to leave school.

This was easier said than done, of course. There were several factors standing in my way: the law, for instance, and the borough council, my parents and teachers. My friends weren't too supportive either, which was odd because I hadn't known them long, but they seemed in the main to want me to stick around. Either that or they didn't see why I should escape seven years of educational servitude if they couldn't. But it wasn't education that I wanted to escape, it was something much more threatening. I had to leave school, or my mother would suffer a hideous fate.

I'd always been a swotty kind of a kid. From my first day at infants' school, sitting cross-legged on the floor by the piano while Miss Badcock played 'Morning Has Broken', watching as she struck the keys and they disappeared and reappeared like miraculously regrowing teeth, I knew that school and I were going to get along.

Children weren't meant to enjoy it, of course. I had an older brother, so I knew before I started that school was only there to make you miserable; it was the grown-up world's way of putting an end to your fun. And I could sort of see that getting up early every day was a pain, but other than that, school was all the things I liked under one roof – friends and books and interesting new things. I learned Indian songs and how to make butter in a jam jar, I had a go at acting, failed to master the flute or the eight times table, wrote poems for the school magazine, and discovered that it didn't matter if you tripped over while French skipping as long as you could laugh about it afterwards. The primary years were peaceful and happy. I passed the eleven-plus exam and got into the local grammar school that everyone wanted their daughters to go to. Mum and Dad were delighted.

Two weeks before I was due to start there though, with the blazer bought and the pencils sharpened, we went away on holiday. What happened has been mentioned elsewhere in this book, but to save you leafing through, I'll reiterate. On a picnic by a river, my dad almost drowned. He didn't die, but it was a damned close-run thing. Grandpa, however, wasn't so lucky. He'd been in hospital recovering from a heart attack when we'd left, but the doctors had assured us he'd be fine, that he'd be sent home soon, that there was nothing at all to worry about, and he himself insisted we should go. So we did. Mum rang him every day to make sure he was OK, and each time he sounded stronger. Then two days after Dad's near miss, Grandpa abruptly died.

It seemed to me that a pattern was emerging. Death had it in for my family. He'd tried to take Dad but Dad had got away. He'd taken Grandpa out of revenge, and now, with the score at one all, Death was out to win. He was obviously coming after Mum. I can't state too strongly how clear this was to me. I knew, just *knew* that Mum was in danger, but nobody else seemed to be aware of it. With all the grief and shock, the rushing back from holiday and making funeral arrangements, they were all too upset and preoccupied to see the bigger picture.

As a result, Mum was wantonly engaging in all kinds of reckless activities – going in cars, crossing roads, climbing stairs, eating pieces of fruit small enough to choke her – as if no harm could come from them. I was mystified by what a daredevil she'd suddenly become, and I didn't like it one little bit. She couldn't be trusted to look after herself, and Dad – a man who'd almost perished in a paddling accident, for God's sake – clearly couldn't be trusted to look after her either. Teenage brothers are teenage brothers, there was no point trying to get him on my side. So it had to be me; I had to protect her myself. I didn't know how I was going to do that, but I did know one thing – I couldn't do it if I was at school.

Looking back, it's all so obvious. What had happened to Dad and Grandpa had combined with nervousness about big school, worries about growing up and yes, a fear of death, to form the perfect breeding ground for anxiety. But this was the Seventies. Kids didn't suffer from anxiety; they just 'made a fuss' and needed to 'pull themselves together'. My parents were as liberal and caring as could be, but even they didn't really get it. The first they knew there was a problem was when the tummy aches began.

At first, there was no consistent pattern. I'd wake up feeling fine, go to school on the bus with my friend and then suddenly, for some reason, become aware that Mum was out somewhere, doing who knew what, and that something terrible might happen to her. I'd feel sick, my stomach would hurt, and I'd need to go to the medical room. Once I was there, I'd lie on the hard bed, looking at the clock on the wall. I'd wonder if she was home yet, imagine the car in a ditch, and agonise over whether Dad would be able to contact me from the hospital. On a different day, the symptoms would start when I woke up. There'd be an hour or so of crying, wailing, retching and writhing before Dad would bundle me in the car and drop me at school. By then it was a *fait accompli*, there was no point in fighting it anymore, and I'd go on to have a perfectly nice day.

Parents and teachers alike were bewildered – some thought I was attention-seeking, others put it down to 'growing pains', but everyone thought it would go away. It's not, after all, unusual for kids to have trouble adjusting to secondary school. My work seemed fine, I wasn't being bullied, so it all just got swept under the carpet. I don't remember it being discussed much by the teachers and I didn't want to raise it. My parents did talk to me about it, but I knew that if I said what was worrying me, they'd just try to reassure me. I genuinely believed Mum was in danger, and that only I could save her; I didn't *want* to be reassured. I wasn't bothered about my own discomfort, or how unhappy I was making everybody else. I could only see the end result on each particular day – avoiding school if possible, keeping Mum in my sights. After a while, there were no stomach pains, not really. And I was only being sick because I'd shoved my fingers down my throat. But I didn't feel any remorse. This was a matter of life or death, and if they made me go into school, I didn't want to think what might happen.

Throughout the first term, things got steadily worse: most days I went in, but would end up in the sick room; some days I didn't go in at all. Every morning, I would wake the household with my whimpers like some morose cockerel. After a while, I took to hurling my school shoes out of my bedroom window, reasoning that no one would send me out of the house barefoot.

My parents were at their wits' end. They took me to the doctor, who prescribed diazepam, but Mum threw them away. She may not have had a better solution, but she'd seen enough of the Sixties to know she didn't want to put her child on pills.

Looking back on it now, it's all a blurry memory, though not, I imagine, as blurry as it might have been had I taken the diazepam. It was becoming apparent that this wasn't going away and by the time I finally did explain my fears to my parents, it had gone on so long that I was beyond reassurance and logic. The anxiety had become a habit, as it so often does. I'd forgotten how to be any other way.

Hoping a complete change might be the solution, Mum and Dad asked if I might be transferred to a school closer to home. The obvious place was only a mile away, but it was the school my mum had gone to and hated, which was why I hadn't been sent there in the first place. We were all getting desperate though, something had to change, and even I thought that a new school might do the trick.

Before a transfer could be agreed, I had to be assessed by an educational psychologist. There were three sessions, as far as I recall, each one held in a dull Victorian municipal building that felt like a doctor's surgery and had the same dispiriting decor and smell.

In the first session, I was given a kind of exam. Part of it consisted of straightforward verbal reasoning, not unlike the questions in the eleven-plus. 'Best is to good as worst is to ...' that kind of thing. I actually rather enjoyed them. There were also common-sense questions that were, I suppose, designed to see how I coped with the world around me, relationships, responsibilities, ethics and so on. I was asked what I would do if my mother cut herself while cooking dinner, to which I replied 'get a plaster or call an ambulance' and got a tick in one of the columns. I imagine if your answer was 'smear myself in her blood and dance naked in the street', you got put in a different column. But to be honest, even if you'd thought it, it wasn't hard to work out that you shouldn't say it out loud.

In the next assessment, I was asked about my life. Particularly close interest was shown to the fact that I sucked my thumb and still slept with a doll. But lots of the eleven-year-old girls I knew sucked their thumbs, and all of them slept with dolls, so I felt rather aggrieved that I was the only one being judged for it. I also wondered how relevant it all was. After all, if you were looking for evidence that I wasn't like other children, the fact that I'd taken to throwing my shoes out of the window seemed like a pretty good starting point.

In the final session, I was seen with Mum and Dad. After a lot of questions and nervous answers and uncomfortable pauses while the psychologist made notes and we all tried to read her writing upside down, we were told that there didn't seem to be anything wrong with me. Educationally and emotionally I was, it appeared, tickety-boo. A1. A perfectly normal child from a perfectly normal family. Mum and Dad were clearly relieved. They'd found the whole process stressful, even a bit humiliating. After all, only months before we'd been the kind of family you saw on the cover of Ladybird books, smiling cheerily as we clambered over a stile on some idyllic outing. I think I was probably the first to realise that this clean bill of health wasn't entirely helpful. None of my friends was locked in a daily battle with the Grim Reaper. Even I wouldn't have called that 'normal'. Of course there was something wrong with me, they just hadn't found out what it was yet.

As things were drawing to a close, and with none of us any the wiser, the psychologist asked if we had any questions. Mum and Dad shook their heads, and said they didn't think so, but they'd been sitting in the waiting room for most of the time I was being assessed, so they didn't know what had been discussed. I didn't really want to ask her anything either. I was pretty keen to get the hell out of there. But it seemed to me that maybe there was something she should have asked me. I honestly didn't want to seem pushy, but with all the written tests and questions about cuddly toys and why it wasn't a good idea to put your hand into a fire, she hadn't actually got around to asking me what was on my mind. I half thought maybe that was how this process worked, but on the off-chance it wasn't, I mentioned it. She flicked back through her notes, as if she was sure we must have covered this already, but not finding anything, she looked a little flustered and asked me what I wanted to say.

I told her how Dad had nearly drowned right there in front of us, how Grandpa had had a heart attack and died, and how I'd had to start big school days after the funeral. I told her about Death stalking the family; that if I turned my back on

Mum, he would get her too. And I told her that I kind of knew this wasn't true any more, because Mum and Dad had explained it to me, but that didn't stop me being frightened and imagining horrible things. I apologised if it looked like I'd been keeping this stuff back; it was just that the time had never seemed quite right to say it. She scribbled a few notes, and agreed that a change of school might be for the best.

Looking back on this whole process, I'm very struck by what I don't remember. I don't remember being offered any counselling. I don't remember anyone giving my parents advice on how to deal with me. I don't think it was the psychologist's fault. Her role was diagnostic not therapeutic. She probably didn't have the time or resources to do anything more than check me over and certify that I was fit for school. We went back home and things carried on as before.

I was now in a holding pattern. With my problems untreated and as bad as ever, it was reluctantly agreed by my parents, the teachers at the original school and me that I may as well stay home until a place became available at the new school. As Mum was a teacher herself, the only thing to be done was for her to take compassionate leave from work and try to keep my education going as best she could. I had, to all intents and purposes, got what I wanted. I was at home all day and every day with my mum. I should have been happy, or at least relieved.

But my God, being home schooled was dull. For a start everyone was miserable. Mum was under threat of losing her job, which we really couldn't afford. Dad was permanently grumpy. He's never really got to grips with mental health problems – even now when we're out somewhere he frequently steers me towards lifts, and when I remind him that I've been claustrophobic most of my life, he'll say, 'But it's a *big* lift.' And my brother was cross with me too, largely because he'd been moaning for years about school and nobody was offering to let him stay home.

Every day we ploughed through worksheets and spelling tests, maths exercises and science books. It was joyless. And because it was all happening at home, everything else became joyless too. Lunchtime and weekends were no more fun than lesson-times. Everything had turned sour. To make matters worse, I was in a class of one – there were no other children. Nobody to play with, nobody to chat to apart from my parents. It was all the bad stuff about school without any of the benefits.

By the time the new school came up with a place for me, I was desperate to get back into mainstream education. My imagination veered wildly between dream scenarios in which I was happy, laughing, studious and popular, and nightmare ones in which I was back in the sick room unable to get through the day. In an unguarded moment, my mum had let slip that this transfer was a last chance; if I couldn't settle this time, the local authority would put me in a 'special unit' for school refusers. I didn't know what a 'special unit' was – I don't think she did either – but I knew from the way she said it that it wasn't special in a good way. Gradually, the nightmare visions overtook the dream ones. I started to expect my own failure. I was so terrified that I wouldn't be able to go to this school either that it looked like becoming a self-fulfilling prophecy.

On the first day of the new term, Mum and I had been told to report to the headteacher's office at the new school shortly after assembly.

The head was a genial, sweet, birdlike lady. She welcomed me and my mother, gave us tea and biscuits, then handed over to her lieutenant, the deputy head Miss Dyson, to introduce me to my new class. But as we left the head's office, it became clear to me that I was now expected to say goodbye to Mum. I couldn't do it. All the terror came back to me – I knew with absolute certainty that if I waved her off now I would never see her again. I started to cry, then shout, then fight. Mum was beside herself and too exhausted to take any kind of control. She'd used up all her resources; she had nothing else to offer. At that moment, I think we both thought the game was up. I was never going to school again.

Miss Dyson, however, had other ideas. She was around fifty years old, tall and slim, a firm face and a no-nonsense air, but quietly sympathetic, even when the tussle to get me away from Mum became physical. Eventually, noticing a small huddle of girls gathering to watch this hysterical small creature attacking their deputy head, she took us both into her office.

And this is where my life turned around.

Miss Dyson, it became clear, wanted two things from this conversation: information and a solution, and she struck me as a woman who got what she wanted. She listened carefully as Mum and I explained all the old stuff yet again – the nasty experiences, the fear, the habitual behaviour. Then she asked us other questions, all about us and me and what I liked doing and what jobs my parents did and what our lives had been like before all this nonsense had taken hold.

She thought for a few moments and then quietly came up with a radical plan. Having discovered that Mum wrote children's stories, she offered her the chance to work on one right there in the school library. Her reasoning was this: I couldn't be panicky about Mum if she was in the same building as me. But equally, it wasn't a good idea for me to start off at this new school with my mother in tow. I'd already been seen behaving outlandishly in the corridor; it would be all too easy to get a reputation as a scaredy-cat. So this way, Mum could be on the premises doing something rather glamorous, and I'd get to have her in school with me without any loss of face.

It was simple, brilliant and, most importantly, it worked. I was taken to meet my new classmates, and Miss Dyson put the word out that my mum was a 'famous' author who was writing a book in the school library. Nobody seemed to question it – certainly nobody teased me about it. If anything, they seemed to think it was pretty cool. And there was another, somewhat unexpected, result of all this: the girls who'd witnessed my meltdown in the school corridor spread the rumour that I'd kicked Miss Dyson. Far from being cast as a vulnerable little victim, my panicky tussle had been misinterpreted as proof that I was 'hard'. I had accidentally become notorious. I was the girl you didn't want to mess with.

It took less than a week for me to settle at the school. I told Mum that I didn't need her with me any more. I knew I was going to be fine. After all, if I did have any problems, Miss Dyson would be there to help.

It was over. Mum went back to work, the family returned to its happy normality, and I started loving school more than ever before.

Miss Dyson used to invite me to her study every so often for a glass of orange squash and a chat, and to check that everything was OK. At the end of my first term, she gave me a tiny silver teaspoon, because it had, on the end of the handle, a little lion hallmark. 'I've seen you change from a frightened mouse into a fierce lion,' she explained, 'and that's how I hope you'll stay.'

I made her a promise that now that I'd cracked this school business, I intended to make a success of it. I told her I wanted to go to Oxford, and was aiming to be head girl. I did both. It was my way of saying thank you to her.

Years later, I was offered the chance to make a short auto-biographical TV film, and I told the producer this story. We decided to make it, and I played Miss Dyson. She and I had stayed in touch since school and now that I was going to tell our story, I rang her and asked her what she recalled.

'I remember a very frightened little girl with her shoes on the wrong feet,' she began. That was news to me; I suppose it was an impotent protest, a natural extension of throwing them out of the window. It was such a quirky detail that we put it in the film.

And then I asked her about the rumours.

'Some of the girls used to say that I'd kicked you,' I said. 'It must have looked that way when I was struggling to get back to Mum.'

'Oh no, you did, dear,' she replied with her characteristic equanimity.

'I did?' I exclaimed. 'I'm so sorry. All these years I'd thought they'd imagined it.'

'Oh no,' she said again, calmly and with a smile in her voice. 'You did it all right, but only very lightly. It was just a playful little kick.'

I wished that every kid in a crisis, all those scared, vulnerable children hitting out and raging and feeling out of place and hopeless, could meet someone just like Miss Dyson. That's all they'd need, really. A woman who was clear-headed and determined, who could keep her sense of humour even when she'd been kicked in the shins. A woman who didn't see a problem, she simply saw a child.

My life on hold

Bear with me. I'm on hold. I'm seventh in the queue and my call is important to them. So it shouldn't take too long, should it?

Something went wrong today – my bank card was blocked or my internet connection stopped working; a parcel wasn't delivered or an appliance broke down. It's not that I can't remember, it's just that there's always something. Think how peaceful and productive life could be if only everything went right. But it's one irritation after another, an eternal ebb and flow of petty dissatisfactions, each one merging into the next, until frankly, it's hard to tell them apart.

Any minute now a customer advisor is going to ask me about this latest one: the bank card, the broken appliance, whatever the hell *it* was. What went wrong, when did it go wrong and how have I tried to resolve it? That's the most important question. If I haven't satisfactorily completed the trouble-shooting ritual, then the moral high ground will collapse beneath me. All day long I've been rehearsing a tone of righteous indignation and if I don't come across as proactive and efficient, I'll never pull it off. And worse than that, they might start to blame it on me. They're like barristers, these people, listening out for inconsistencies and uncertainties, anything that'll mark me out as flaky. You can hear them thinking, 'She doesn't know what she's talking about. She's a woman. She sounds at least forty. She can't understand technology – not with all those hormones. Never in a million years will it have occurred to her to switch it off and switch it back on again. Because that's our little secret, we in the cabal of experts. She's ballsed it up, it's obviously her fault, and now she's trying to pin it on us.' So I have to be focused. I have to know my facts. And then I can say, with absolute calm conviction, 'I've done what I can. I'm not an idiot. This isn't *my* screw-up, it's *your* screw-up.' Only it would help to know which screw-up I'm talking about.

It could have been my fault, of course. It's entirely possible that I did order the wrong thing or break it or forget to plug it in. And the longer they keep me on hold, the more time I'll have to convince myself that I did. Maybe I should tone down the fury a notch just in case. Maybe I shouldn't call at all. But no, it needs sorting out – whatever *it* is – and until I've done that, I can't carry on with anything else.

And that's the biggest problem of all – the one in my head; the one that lets these trivial inconveniences niggle away at me, and grow and grow until there's no concentration left. That's the thing that really needs fixing. Only I'm pretty sure my brain is out of warranty. But no. It's not my screw-up, it's their screw-up. Stick to the facts, hold on to the anger. This is my moment. My chance for a sliver of redemption. Well, it will be when somebody answers the phone.

I'm tenth in the queue, and my call is hugely important to them. Tenth? Wasn't I …? Never mind. I'm in a queue, so it shouldn't be too long now.

I'll just sit here listening to the 'Moonlight Sonata' played on a stylophone, drawing moustaches on eminent people in the newspaper. When was the last time they were left on hold? Presumably, if you're rich or successful, you can hire someone to do your holding for you. What luxury that would be. I honestly can't think of anything better – forget mansions and private jets, if someone could just call customer services for me every time I needed them, I'd be happy. But no, we ordinary Joes have to waste our own precious time. And it is precious. It takes so long to make a complaint that you can't just do it in a redundant five minutes while you're waiting for a bus or folding up the washing. You have to set aside one of those rare oases of quiet solitude, when you know you won't be interrupted by kids or the boss or the doorbell – the one time, in fact, which could be spent reading poetry or walking in a sun-dappled meadow or falling in love – and instead spend it listening to muzak and selecting option two.

Ah, a voice. An automated voice. There's a higher-than-average volume of calls at this time of day, she tells me. I might want to log onto their website.

I allow myself a mirthless laugh into the telephonic void. That website, that time-wasting, blood-pressure-raising, useless bloody website. I know it all too well. If I had nothing better to do with my life, I'd be on hold now just to complain about the website. I remember once, when I was young and guileless, about an hour and a half ago, thinking that it might be easier to sort out … whatever *it* is … online. That website promised a

89

world of opportunity – you could make a purchase, pay a bill, view other products and services, even look at pictures of the board of directors if you had a mind to do so, all at the click of a link. What you couldn't do was sort out my problem. For that, it seemed, you had to speak to an Actual Human Being. So I began to search for a phone number. I tried the Home page and it took me to the Contact Us page. That took me to the Report a Problem page and that, in turn, back to the Home page. I tried again: Home page, Help page, Help page, Contact Us page, like some mad cyberspace whirligig. Finally, and with the utmost reluctance, the website coughed up a phone number. I spoke to an Actual Human Being. He seemed surprised. Had I tried their website, he wondered? Because most people found it a faster way to deal with … whatever it was. Still, now that I was on the line, he was certain he could help. He just needed to speak to his supervisor. And that, I dimly recall, is how I came to be on hold.

I'm twenty-third in the queue now, which definitely doesn't sound right. But my call is ridiculously important to them. So I suppose I'll hang on just a little bit longer.

A call centre is the court of a tyrant king. He'll keep you waiting for as long as he wants to, pass you on to as many different people as he fancies. The only power you retain is the right to hang up. But do so, and you'll have to go through the whole ordeal again tomorrow. So you won't. You'll stay on the line like I do, fruitlessly explaining your problem again and again to every fresh voice you hear.

It's the new form of confession – Father, I have sinned, or rather you have, but you'll try to make out it's my fault. And with it comes the modern catechism – the interrogative creed of security questions. What's your date of birth? What is the first line of your address? Your postcode? Your mother's maiden name? Your pet's name? The name of your school? Your college? Your oldest cousin? Your favourite teacher? It's an endless quest for self-validation, as if any of us needed another one of those.

'We just need to confirm who you are,' they say. 'It shouldn't take a moment.'

And you wonder, if that's true, why Sartre made such heavy weather of it.

The music changes. A Vivaldi adagio to calm me down. My call is ludicrously important to them. And I'm forty-sixth in the queue, now, so there's definitely been some movement ...

I'm angry, and the next person I speak to is going to feel my wrath. They don't know who they're messing with. I've got a career and qualifications. I can cook and drive a car. I'm a mother – hell, I've created two whole people. I'm not going to be defeated by a customer services operative. But that wouldn't be fair. They're just another lab rat in the same social experiment as me, only much worse off, because while I'm shouting at them for taking me away from my day job, their day job is being shouted at by people like me.

I need to relax. I shouldn't let it get to me. I need to take a more measured approach to these things. Stuff happens, and when it does it needs to be fixed. I'm a grown-up; I must take responsibility, and with great responsibility comes great inconvenience. All this waiting and repetition and jumping through hoops – I shouldn't take it personally. But the trouble is, it *is* personal. This bank card that's been wrongly blocked is *my* bank card, the broken appliance is *my* broken appliance. And when I ring to talk to an Actual Human Being, I want to be treated like an Actual Human Being. Not shunted from one phone bank to another, as if I had nothing more pressing to do with my time than to float around the ether howling in impotent rage. If I ruled the world, I'd make customer service all about serving the customer, and not about fobbing them off. But I never will rule the world; I'll never fully reach my potential in any area, and neither will you. This is my career now, this is how I spend my days: confirming my date of birth, spelling my mother's maiden name, and pressing the bloody hash key.

I'm lost in a queue. My call means nothing to them. My life is on hold. But I'll hang on just in case.

I want you to relax

You can't go through your life being as anxious and phobia-ridden as me without somebody, at some point, suggesting hypnotherapy. People suggest all kinds of things, of course – sometimes because they think it might genuinely help you, often just to shut up your endless self-indulgent wittering so that they can talk about something else for a change. But the reason hypnotherapy gets mentioned a lot is that many people believe it's changed their lives.

I never thought hypnosis would be for me; I'm too much of a control freak. It took me months to get used to driving an automatic car. I just couldn't be sure that this unseen power, silently deciding when I should move up from third gear to fourth, wouldn't suddenly go rogue, plunge me into reverse and send me hurtling backwards down a motorway. So how could I possibly hand over control of my mind?

Years ago, I was taken to see a stage hypnotist. It was the usual cavalcade of people barking like dogs and waving their arms around helplessly whenever a trigger word was said. And all I could think was why would you let someone do that to you? Why would losing control and doing something eminently ridiculous in public be anyone's idea of a good night out? Which explains why I never took drugs, but not why I got into acting.

Most of the time, my anxieties are a quiet inconvenience. They don't stop me being a mother or a wife or an actor or enjoying the things I really want to enjoy, and the only person they're troubling is me. But every so often, say once every five or ten years, a little outbreak will occur, several anxieties collide in a kind of perfect storm, and after a few sleepless nights I'll decide to do something about it. When that happens, I can't help feeling that if somebody could indeed just take control of my troubled, churning, boiling sea of a mind and turn it into a millpond, that really would be quite nice actually.

Yes, you can do it yourself; you can take pills, which I prefer not to do (see earlier paragraph – control freakery), or you can see a therapist, which I have done with some success. But it takes time and effort, and sometimes those sleepless nights make you yearn for the simple, effective, short, sharp solution that hypnotherapy might provide.

So it is that twice I've succumbed to temptation.

The first time, the children were very young, and I'd taken a part in a television series that meant going away from them for ten days. There were of course practical difficulties to sort out, so Phil and I worked our way through everything, and before long we had sorted out our childcare, our back-up childcare, the kids' food and the kids' back-up food, the food for the people doing childcare and the back-up food for the back-up people doing childcare. And anyway, Phil was going to be home every night. We explained to the children that Mummy would be back soon, that it was just a few days, and that there might even be some presents in my suitcase when I got home, and everybody was happy.

Then, a couple of nights before I was due to leave I woke up in the cold sweat of all-out panic: what was I THINKING? These were my CHILDREN. My BABIES. I had carried them inside my body for nine months, and now, a mere five years later, I was LEAVING them? To the mercy of GOD KNEW WHAT? WHAT KIND OF A MONSTER WAS I?

I got out of bed and put the kettle on, genuinely thinking that a cup of tea might make everything all right. But it didn't, so I poured myself a brandy. That didn't help either. I lay on the sofa and tried some deep-breathing exercises. Breathe in ... two ... three ... four ... and out ... two ... three ... four. And in ... two ... and I wouldn't mind ... four ... but I have to fly ... two ... three ... four ... on a plane ... two ... a bloody plane ... four ... what if it crashes ... two ... three ... four ... will they even remember me ... two ... three ... four ... maybe it's for the best ... two ... three ... four ... maybe Phil would marry someone less neurotic ... two ... three ... four ... and the kids wouldn't grow up to be a total mess like their mother ... two ... three ... This really wasn't working.

Now I was in uncharted waters. I'd tried all my usual tricks (pre-therapy I didn't know they were called 'strategies', and even post-therapy I'm not sure 'having a drink and gasping for air' is really worthy of the name) and nothing was making it any better. There was one thought going through my mind: nothing on God's earth was going to make me get on that plane and leave my children. And that, as far as I was concerned, was that.

In the morning, I made breakfast, got the children to school and rang my agent, trying to sound like the rational, professional human being he'd been dealing with all these years.

'Hi darling, all good, all good. Everything, you know ... good. Erm, this TV series? ... I know, *so* exciting. Really great. Just out of interest, what would be the position if ... say ... you know ... I *couldn't* do it?'

I knew the answers already, of course, (letting people down, breach of contract, reputation in tatters, never work in this town again, etc, etc) but I needed someone else to say them, because whenever I said them to myself, all I could hear was 'BUT WHAT IF I DIE AND NEVER SEE MY CHILDREN AGAIN?'

I knew I had to go. I wanted to go. I just didn't know how the hell I was going to be able to. My agent, who had after all elected to spend his working life managing actors, and had therefore had to deal with all manner of crises over the years, was surprisingly sanguine.

'Listen,' he said patiently, 'this happens more often than you might think. People take on work and then suddenly panic that they can't do it ... maybe because it's a theatre role and they haven't been on stage for years, or maybe because they have personal problems and they don't think they'll be able to focus. It's fine. You're fine. And I know someone who can help.' And he gave me the number of a hypnotherapist. It was Wednesday lunchtime; I was due at the airport Friday morning. I dialled the number without hesitation.

Her name was Veronica, and for someone in a therapeutic role, her phone manner was unexpectedly brisk.

'No I'm sorry, I have no appointments at all for the rest of the week,' she said. I could hear the 'no appointments' part in her voice, but the 'sorry' aspect wasn't really coming across. I threw myself on her mercy, told her how effusive my agent had been about her abilities, explained that I was in a dreadful state and desperately needed some help to get me through the next few days. Eventually, and with a weary sigh, she replied, 'Well, I suppose you could come at five, but I have to be at a supper party at seven, so it won't be a full session.'

I thanked her profusely, promised I would do my best to snap out of my trance in plenty of time for the canapés, and set off to the appointment.

Veronica's practice was in a swanky-looking mansion block in Chelsea. She opened the door, already dressed for the evening – a shirt dress and court shoes, pearlescent nails, groomed rather than glamorous, her hair set, sprayed, immoveable. She ushered me into the sitting room, which was similarly well presented – plump sofas that looked as though no one was allowed to sit on them, and antique Chinese table lamps somewhat pointlessly casting little pools of light onto themselves. I offered up yet more apologies and thanks, and the more she said it was fine, that she was glad to help, the less she sounded like she meant it. She didn't seem like a woman who was comfortable around the needy; perhaps she'd drifted into therapy because all the vacancies for barking at the lower orders had been filled.

She ushered me towards a wing-backed chair, surreptitiously set a small alarm clock on the table next to her own chair, and asked me to explain the problem.

'Well, I've accepted a part – a nice part – in a TV series, but it'll mean leaving my children. Only for a few days really, but ... they're very young and ...' I was beginning to get tearful again. Veronica handed me a tissue, not in a kindly way; probably to protect the upholstery.

'They don't understand, do they?' she said, through pursed lips.

'Well, they're only little. I think they're doing their best.'

'Not the children,' replied Veronica. 'Men. Husbands. They just don't get it.'

I was confused. I hadn't even mentioned my husband.

'You should have just said to him: "I'm not ready to go back to work, yet, chum. I may never be ready. You made me have these children ... you can't blame me for wanting to stay home with them."'

'I think you may have misunderstood ...' I ventured.

'I see it time and time again. Young women like you so upset, and their husbands wanting it all their own way.'

'Right, if I can just clarify ...' I interrupted. 'I didn't take the job because he made me. I took it because I'm an actress. And it's a great part. And I haven't worked much since the kids were born ... I've sort of forgotten what it's like to be me.'

It suddenly struck me that that was at the root of it, and for a moment I wondered if that was Veronica's strategy – to get me to analyse the problem myself by deliberately suggesting it was caused by something else. My God, I thought, that's brilliant. And she hasn't even 'put me under' yet.

'My husband was exactly the same ...' she continued, with the same tight-lipped snarl, and I instantly realised there was no strategy. Veronica was simply imposing on me whatever misery and dissatisfaction she'd experienced. In her eyes, I wasn't a crying woman looking for an answer – I was *all* crying women, a kind of omnivictim. I was, in fact, *her* after the divorce, after he'd run off with that bitch, and before she'd bravely picked herself up, got her hair done and started back on the supper party circuit again.

'So much for feminism,' Veronica continued. 'They've got us exactly where they want us. Looking after the kids *and* earning the money. Well done us.'

'Phil actually works really hard ...' I began to say.

'Does he? That's what he wants you to think.'

'No, he really does. And he's terrific with the children. This really is a problem about me ...'.

'Oh, he's good ...' she murmured in bitter admiration. 'He's got you tied up in knots.'

'No, honestly. I've tied myself up in knots. He's a sweetie. I'm lucky to have him.'

There was a brief, uncomfortable pause, while Veronica appeared to consider the notion that all men might not perhaps be bastards. Then, rejecting it with a neat shake of her head, she announced that she would begin the hypnosis. She walked around the room, turning off the lamps, which made little discernible difference to the lighting or the mood.

'Now, I want you to relax. Close your eyes, focus on taking slow, regular breaths.'

But I couldn't relax, and I couldn't focus on my breathing. All I could think about was the fact that a woman I'd never set eyes on before had just told me the man I loved was a lying, manipulative shit. I was furious. I wanted to leap to his defence, but I'd missed my opportunity. I should have said what I thought of her straightaway, collected my bag and walked out. But I'd left it too late, and by closing my eyes and slowing my breathing, I'd tacitly entered into a contract with her. I was opening the door to my mind and inviting Veronica to come in and make herself at home.

I kept thinking about the stage-show I'd seen – the members of the audience sent out into the world hard-wired to bark every time somebody said the word 'dog'. If a hypnotist could really mess with your head like that, how did I know Veronica wouldn't reprogram mine so that henceforth every time Phil said he loved me, I'd automatically snort with derision and tell him he had a funny way of showing it? I decided that the only safe option was to close my mind, refuse to succumb. Outwardly, I did everything she asked me to do, but inside I was saying the alphabet backwards, and reciting times tables. I wondered if she would know, if there was some way that hypnotists had of discerning a genuine trance from a fake one. But she seemed oblivious to it. I think she was more concerned about getting to her party on time, because when, at one point, I squinted at her through half-opened eyes, she was re-tying the belt on her dress and checking her nail polish.

Eventually, it was over. I yawned somewhat ostentatiously, stretched my arms up and said it had been amazing. I felt as though I'd forfeited my right to be honest with her, and it was easier just to play along. I don't think she was bothered anyway, but in the spirit of professionalism, she asked, 'And how do you feel about getting on that plane and leaving your children now?'

'Oh, much better,' I lied. 'I really think I can do it.'

She looked at me, with one eyebrow arched, and I thought she was on to me. Then she leant forward conspiratorially and said, 'For what it's worth, I don't think you can cope.'

I was baffled. It was as if a car mechanic had said, 'Well, I've given it a full service, but if I'm honest, it's still a death trap.' Was she acknowledging the session had been a failure, or simply dismissing me as a lost cause?

'No really,' I said. 'I think I'll be OK now.' I was still lying, of course, but it was no longer about being polite. We were locked in a quite bizarre power game. I'd gone to see Veronica feeling helpless. She'd made me feel not just helpless but hopeless, and the only way I could claw back a little self-respect was to tell her what a great job she'd done. It had cost me £50 to emerge feeling terrible, it would have cost her nothing to shake me by the hand, wish me luck and tell me she was sure it would all work out. But for whatever reasons, she couldn't find it in herself to do it. Instead, as she folded my cheque neatly and tucked it into her purse, she said, 'Well, if I were you, I wouldn't get on that plane. Big mistake.'

And that was how we left it.

When I walked through my front door, Phil was standing in the hallway holding an envelope.

'How did it go?' he asked.

'Useless. What's in the envelope?'

'Plane tickets. For me and the kids. I thought it might help if we came too. Just for the first couple of days. Once you're into the job, you'll be fine.'

I put my arms around him.

'I'd love her to meet you,' I said.

* * *

For a long time after my session with Veronica, I dismissed hypnotherapy as a waste of time and money. And anyway, I didn't need it. As Phil had predicted, once he and the kids had got me on that plane, I was instantly back into the swing of working, and they'd been able to come home and leave me happily engrossed in what I was doing. When I returned, to stop such a crisis happening again, I'd taken a course of cognitive behavioural therapy, which started from the reassuring premise that since I was the one making myself stressed, I was also the one who could make myself calm again. It worked pretty well, and things had jogged along pretty well ever since.

But then, some years later, when I began to feel the claustrophobia getting worse again, I thought I might give hypnosis another go. I'd always felt as though, for all the improvements cognitive therapy had brought me, the wiring in my brain that told me to be scared of confined spaces had stubbornly remained in place. It was just that sometimes it was easier than others to bypass it. Maybe a good hypnotherapist could get in there and actually put the wiring right.

Hannah came highly recommended, but then so had Veronica, so I turned up for my appointment in a spirit of scepticism. She was young, blonde and very pretty and wore severe black glasses, which I suspected she didn't actually need and was just wearing so that people would take her seriously.

We had a long preliminary chat during which, I was relieved to note, she refrained from telling me that my problems were all the fault of my husband. In fact, she pointed out that they were nobody's 'fault', that it wasn't especially helpful to think that they were, and that yes, she was sure she could help me.

'Right, shall we give this a go?' she asked, and I said I supposed we might as well.

I lay down on a sort of recliner, covered myself, at Hannah's suggestion, with a distractingly stylish rug, tried not to wonder where she'd bought it and closed my eyes.

'Now look,' she said, 'there's no right way and wrong way with hypnotherapy.'

I wanted to beg to differ, to tell her about Veronica, but I let her carry on uninterrupted.

'You might go to sleep, you might stay wide awake. You might not even want to keep your eyes closed. Your breathing can be deep or shallow. All I ask is that you listen to what I'm saying to you. Beyond that, it's all up for grabs.'

She started off on her monologue; it was the usual relaxation stuff I'd heard a million times in drama classes and on self-help recordings – lots of references to floating and clouds and happy places and babbling brooks. I lay there wishing that her therapy room wasn't so close to a building site. But after a while the sound of drilling and sawing subsided – perhaps it was the builders' lunchbreak – and even the traffic outside seemed to shut up for a while.

Hannah carried on talking for a bit longer. She knew I wasn't asleep, and every now and then she'd ask me to raise an arm or turn my foot or something, and I complied quite happily, wondering what was the point of it all.

Much sooner than I'd anticipated, she began bringing me back to the surface, or however she described it, and I figured that this was just a quick try-out for my first session and, with a certain amount of relief, opened my eyes.

I remember noticing the traffic noise, and thinking how lucky we were that it hadn't been that loud when I was trying to relax. The building work had started up again too.

'Did you feel yourself in a deep state of relaxation?' Hannah asked. I couldn't see any point in lying, so I just said, 'No. Sorry.'

'That's OK,' she said.

I explained that it wasn't that I hadn't felt relaxed, just that it didn't feel any different from any other deep-breathing exercise I'd done.

'That's really fine,' she said again, and I waited to see what she would do with the rest of the session, but when she started talking about whether I wanted to come again, and flicking through her diary, I realised that she felt we'd gone as far as we could go for one day. Now, I didn't mind this except that ... well, you know ... if you're paying for an hour, you expect to get an hour.

Hannah must have sensed my confusion, because she suddenly asked, 'How long did that feel like it took? I mean, how long do you think you were lying there?'

'About ten minutes, maybe fifteen. I assume you end it sooner if it's not, you know, taking effect.'

'It was forty-five minutes,' she said smiling and looking, I couldn't help noticing, a tiny bit smug.

I got my phone out of my bag and looked at the time. The hour was up. I suddenly felt rather unsettled.

'That building work next door ...' I began.

'Yes, I'm sorry about that. There's nothing I can do, I'm afraid. I just have to hope my clients can screen it out.'

'I thought it had stopped,' I said. 'And the traffic. I thought it had just gone a bit quiet.'

Hannah tried unsuccessfully to suppress another smile.

'So what do you think? Is it worth another session?' she asked.

A week later I was back on the recliner. I'd been looking forward to coming. I'd told everyone I'd met about the freakish time-shift in our first session, the magical silencing of London traffic, the overwhelming calm I'd carried with me for the rest of that day. I had decided that this was going to work. I liked Hannah. She'd even told me where I could buy the rug.

I closed my eyes, and listened to her voice. I felt instantly calmer. Today was the day my claustrophobia was going to melt away. If only my knee didn't itch. Maybe I could just scratch it. Hell, of course I could. She'd said, hadn't she, that it didn't matter if I was wide awake? Well, I was, and my knee was itchy. But as soon as I'd scratched it, I could go back to that lovely, calming, quiet place. There. That was better. Much, much better. Now I could concentrate on relaxing. And breathing. Deep, slow breathing. If only I didn't have that tickle in my throat, I could really breathe deeply. Maybe I should try to clear it. Just a little cough. It seemed wrong somehow, to break the moment with a big, loud throat clear, but I couldn't really breathe as deeply as ... I couldn't really breathe. OK, I had to clear my throat now. It was a compulsion. Maybe I could do it quietly, unknowingly, like someone in a trance might do it. How would someone in a trance clear their throat? Maybe the very act of clearing it was proof that you weren't in a trance. I needed to know that actually, because what if I had to play the part of a person *pretending* to be in a trance sometime, and I could use a little throat clear to signal to the audience that the character was faking. Maybe I should ask Hannah about it. Oh hang on, she's busy hypnotising someone. Oh yes. Oh bugger. It's me.

We'd reached the point in the process where Hannah was describing being in a lift, getting me to visualise the doors closing, the sound of the machinery, the closeness of the walls. She asked me to tell her how anxious it made me feel from one to ten. Ten, I told her. She carried on guiding me through images of myself in that lift feeling calm, complete, able to cope with my environment. I listened to everything she said but the building site next door seemed so much louder than before. And however much I tried to imagine a confident, smiling me taking pleasure in this effortless lift ride, what I kept seeing was a sweating, gasping, panicking me screaming for someone to let her out.

'How anxious do you feel about the lift now?' Hannah asked, and I knew I was meant to say zero or one, but I couldn't in all conscience say I felt any better than the first time she asked me. It was pointless lying, I realised that, but she was working so hard. And if it hadn't been for that damn itch and my throat and the building site and the traffic, maybe it would have worked. I thought for a second, and then, in the sort of woozy voice I thought I might use if I ever got to play that character pretending to be in a trance, I murmured, 'Six.' Hannah sounded delighted, so delighted that I instantly wished I'd gone for a more conservative number, say, eight. But it was too late now; she thought she'd worked wonders, and it wasn't her fault that she hadn't.

She slowly brought me back from the trance-like state that I hadn't actually been in, and I opened my eyes, sat up and did the same ostentatious yawn and stretch that I'd done with Veronica. Nothing was any better than it had been before, not even my acting.

'Well, that went very well,' she said. 'I think we made real progress.'

I felt dreadful, even though the only person I'd cheated was myself.

'How do you feel about giving it another go next week?'

'Er ... yes,' I said vaguely. 'I'll need to check my diary ...'

'Of course. And if we do, I think we might want to try a little challenge. Now that your anxiety level is so much lower, what if I meet you at reception and we come up together in the lift?'

I was busy the following week, and the week after that. I never went back to see Hannah, even though that first session had given me a tantalising glimpse of how hypnotherapy might work. I'd wanted someone to rewire my brain, just a little. But instead, I'd rewired it myself, tangling up the cause of my claustrophobia with the additional anxiety of not wanting to let people down. I still don't use lifts and it's a bloody nuisance. But maybe I just need to relax about it. After all, how hard can a little relaxation be?

Untrained melody

There was a caretaker at my school who could play the spoons. I don't remember how this news first got out, but once it did it spread like billy-o, and we were determined to see it with our own eyes. So one morning before school started, a large group of us crammed into a classroom. There was a buzz of anticipation as we waited for him to turn up. Well, we were young, none of us had discovered drugs yet, and someone we knew was about to play music with cutlery – damn right we were excited.

Moments before the bell went, the caretaker strolled in, climbed onto one of the desks and, with great solemnity, produced from his inside jacket pocket a couple of spoons. A hush descended. He played 'Any Old Iron' followed by 'My Old Man's a Dustman' – the only two songs anybody ever plays on the spoons, but no less thrilling if you've never heard them before. The man was a genius, a virtuoso. There was this clickety-clackety bit, followed by a knock, knock, knockety, knock, and a light sprinkle of brrrrippps. It was a tableware triumph. And because the spoons – however skilfully played

– are essentially percussive rather than melodic, he sang too. Well, he had to really: since both songs are broadly similar, we'd never have known when to applaud otherwise. But I like to imagine that of all the performances he ever gave, this was the most warmly received. He made a little bow and carefully replaced his instruments in his pocket, ready to be used for the next recital, or for tea and a yoghurt, whichever came first. Then he clambered down from the desk and went away to bleed some radiators.

Music, especially that sort of unrehearsed, untrained, spontaneous music was a huge part of my childhood. My dad had a beautiful jazzy tenor voice, and for a brief period before I was born he'd stumbled, without any particular ambition, into being a crooner with an upmarket dance band. The thing that marked him out, I'm told, was his uncanny impersonation of Danny Kaye, complete with quirky gestures and machine-gun delivery. By the time we kids came along, he'd consigned 'The Ugly Duckling' to the back of a drawer marked 'faintly embarrassing' and when dewy-eyed elderly aunts referred to it, he'd swiftly move the conversation on. The singing, though, continued (albeit not for public consumption), and often, while hanging the washing on the line, he'd produce a top-notch rendition of 'That Old Black Magic' for an audience of sparrows.

I loved singing too, and it turned out I had a peculiar knack. When a song was playing on the radio, even if I'd never heard it before, I'd find myself singing a harmony to it. It was just the way my brain interpreted the sounds. I thought everybody did it, until a teacher at primary school told me otherwise. I couldn't explain how the harmony worked – to this day I've never mastered any kind of music theory – I just knew when it sounded right. So it was inevitable that Dad and I would often team up, him washing, me drying, while belting out a harmonised 'Fly Me to the Moon'.

In spite of this, we never thought of ourselves as musical. Those people we saw on *Ask the Family*, where Mother and Father were piano teachers and both children were studying for grade eight harpsichord – that wasn't us. None of us could even read music, let alone play an instrument, but there was always singing. Every Friday night, when we lit the Shabbat candles, my dad would sing the kiddush prayer and we'd all join in in four-part harmony. Hebrew a cappella. It was the same at Chanukah and Passover. Nobody ever told us what to do; we just figured out that Jeremy was the bass, Mum the alto, Dad the tenor and me – I filled all the gaps in between. We were like the Von Trapps, only fewer in number and more Semitic. Occasionally a visiting relative would drop by for Friday night dinner, and I'd catch them looking askance, wondering why kiddush had turned into choral evensong. That was when I realised other families didn't behave like us, and I'd feel a bit embarrassed. But the rest of the time, we were blissfully unselfconscious about singing together, which meant that we could be blissfully unselfconscious about singing on our own.

We used to have a recording of a Peter Sellers sketch where a man performs 'All the Things You Are' to himself while shaving. Gradually, his reedy, unaccompanied voice is glorified by the swelling strings of a Hollywood orchestra. Like all great comedy, it says something each of us knows to be true. When I sing in the shower or the car, it's not just one lone voice I'm hearing; it's a full orchestral accompaniment, massed ranks of choristers, and the Nelson Riddle band. I hear a complete, recorded, perfected version of whatever song it is. It's just a shame nobody else can hear it too.

I think perhaps that's why vocal harmony has always appealed to me. If you can't get hold of a band, then a few friends singing with you will have to do. Right through my school days I surrounded myself with girls with tuneful voices. I didn't go as far as auditioning my friends – that would be freakish – and other qualities mattered too, like loyalty, a sense of humour and an Etch A Sketch, since I never had one. But subconsciously, I think, I was searching for that perfect harmonic sound, and the friends who couldn't sing were unintentionally marginalised.

I started a barbershop quartet when I was ten. When I mentioned this to my children they rolled their eyes as if it just confirmed their worst fears about me. And they were right to. Nobody sang barbershop in 1970s Essex, not even barbers, and certainly not ten-year-old girls. But one evening, a dozen or so geeky bow-tie wearers from Yale showed up on *Nationwide*. They performed a close harmony version of the Whiffenpoof Song, and I was inexplicably smitten – not by the young men (who were, may I reiterate, wearing bow ties) but by the sound.

The very next day, I gathered some of my mercifully uncool friends and we began practising. We rehearsed 'I Want a Girl Just Like the Girl That Married Dear Old Dad'. Now that I think about the choice of song, the whole scenario just gets odder and odder. But there we were in our hallway night after night, with me refining harmonies and conducting little vocal swoops and slides. It was these, after all, that would give us the edge over ... well, over any of the other Essex-based, all-female, pre-pubescent barbershop quartets that fate might throw our way. I don't think we ever actually performed it – at least not to any wider audience than our parents and bewildered siblings – but I still recall the pleasure of hearing out loud harmonies that I'd previously only imagined.

Then one glorious evening when I was probably twelve or thirteen, I suddenly hit upon a brilliant idea. I used to write songs for fun – and there was eye-rolling from my kids when I told them that one too. But being unable either to notate music or to accompany myself with an instrument, it was fiendishly difficult to convey to my mum and dad exactly what it sounded like in my head. This was a source of some frustration, though clearly not enough to warrant getting off my lazy arse and learning to play the piano. Anyway, on the evening in question, I had recorded myself on a cassette player singing the melody of my latest ditty, and I was listening to it and singing a harmony at the same time when inspiration struck. If I borrowed my brother's cassette player too, and recorded myself on a second tape singing along with my own voice on the original one, I would have a multi-tracked two-part harmony. And then, of course, if I taped myself singing along with *that* I could have three-parts, four-parts, as many harmonies as I could come up with, without having to wait for my friends to finish their homework and cycle over. It worked, after a fashion. Each recording degraded slightly in quality as you couldn't help picking up the sounds in the air between me and the microphone. So as the harmonies became more densely layered, they also became more muffled and confusing. Sometimes you could hear Z-*Cars* in the background, or Mum talking to her sister on the phone. But effectively, I had my own barbershop quartet right there in my bedroom, and it was nowhere near as sinister as that sounds.

As I got older, the opportunities to be a part of something musical increased, but they became more formalised, less spontaneous. When the school choir was asked to do a Christmas concert at a local church, I was given a solo. My parents had always had a relaxed attitude to my singing hymns, but none of us was too sure what the matriarch of the family, Grandma Dolly, might think about me standing in front of a Christian altar carolling about the baby Jesus. We needn't have worried. Family is family, and when I got to my feet to sing 'In the Bleak Midwinter', there in the front pew was a small, elderly Jewish lady in red lipstick and an astrakhan coat, dabbing her eyes with a tissue.

I sang my way through school and university and my first few acting jobs still with the same level of idiot confidence I'd had in the kitchen doing the washing up. My hobby became part of my career. I seemed to have stumbled into being a singer just as Dad had, a quarter of a century earlier. The fact that I had no training, and didn't have the first clue about technique only made me more confident. I had no way of knowing if I was doing it wrong. I believed I could do it and although I always half expected them to, nobody ever told me I couldn't. And finally, I landed a part – not a huge one, but I didn't care – in a West End musical.

Sondheim's *Company*, jazzy, rhythmic, full of wilfully complex harmonies, felt like what I'd been aiming for all along. Rehearsals were, quite simply, my dream made real; a glorified extension of harmonising with my mates in the hallway at home. But the apogee of my musical experiences was about to come.

One morning, shortly before we opened, we were all asked to gather for the sitzprobe. I had no idea what this was, and was too embarrassed to ask. With hindsight I'm glad, because the sitzprobe – the first time the orchestra and singers get to perform together – became for me one of the most perfectly spontaneous musical moments of my life. The musicians arrived and did their matter-of-fact musician-stuff: putting instruments together, tightening bits, cleaning other bits, shaking them, blowing through them, tuning them. When everyone was ready, we opened our scores, and for the first time heard the overture played not on a rehearsal piano but by trumpets and strings and woodwind. And as we turned the page the cast joined in. All those years of singing around the house, dreaming I had an orchestra and a full set of harmonising vocals with me and here it was. The real thing. I was Peter Sellers singing 'All the Things You Are' in the bathroom, only all the things he'd wanted were mine.

I should have got out while I was winning. The next job, another Sondheim musical, was a two-hander, and as soon as rehearsals began, I knew I'd overstretched myself. It was just too big a responsibility, and for the first time, I felt exposed. Everyone is, of course, when they sing in public; I had been ever since 'In the Bleak Midwinter' at the Methodist church. But now I was in a show where one half of the cast was a seasoned, trained professional, and the other half was just having a go, giving it her best shot, seeing what happened. Who the hell did I think I was? The reviews were perfectly fine, but I utterly lost my confidence. I had to keep myself going for the rest of the run, and since I no longer believed I was any good, the best I could hope for was to be audible. So I became paranoid about my voice, avoided people with colds, wouldn't go anywhere noisy, in case I strained it trying to be heard. I'd taken the thing I loved and turned it into a chore, a burden, a pain in the arse. I'd never really intended singing to be a job, I just loved making music with people. If I couldn't enjoy it, then I didn't want anything to do with it.

And that was how things stayed for a few years. I barely sang at all, not even at home. I missed it like crazy, but whenever I tried, all I could hear, drowning out the Nelson Riddle Band in my head, were my own limitations.

When I had children, I gradually became aware of some-thing quite unexpected. With so many other things to worry about, music became a spontaneous pleasure all over again. Almost everything you do with a young baby – how you feed them, hold them, put them to sleep – is contentious and fraught with risk. But no one ever tells you not to sing to them. No one says, 'Ooh, watch that B flat. Baby's ears might not be ready for it.' It's broadly accepted to be a good thing. So I did, constantly. I lost all that performance anxiety, and sang to them when they were in the bath and when I was cooking their dinner and when they were settling down to sleep. The question was whether I'd be brave enough to sing in front of an audience of grown-ups ever again.

Then, out of the blue, I was offered a part in a musical, conditional on the director hearing me sing. I hadn't done it for so many years that nobody – least of all me – knew whether I could any more. As it happened, it clashed with another job, but we agreed that I'd go along anyway, just in case it could all be made to work.

I sat in the bar of the theatre with some sheet music – though I still, after all these years, hadn't learned to read it – and I was shaking. Actually shaking. This was a part I'd already been offered, in a show I wasn't free to do – there was only one possible explanation: on the other side of that wall was a group of strangers about to judge me on my singing. All the anxiety had come back to me, and with it the regret that something I'd once found effortless had stopped being any kind of fun.

They called me in, we chatted for a bit, I took a deep breath, leant against the back of the piano to stop myself trembling and went for it.

It turns out if you can sing in a car, you can sing in a rehearsal room. And if you can sing in a rehearsal room, you can sing on a stage. All my nerves, the lack of confidence, the decision to stop doing it for a while were just the result of taking it too seriously. I'm not a 'singer'. Never was and never will be. But like millions of other people, I can knock out a tune if I put my mind to it. And that means that everywhere I go, whatever I'm doing, whether it's in front of an audience or a washing machine, in front of a microphone or my kids, I have music with me, in me – unplanned, instinctive, spontaneous, accidental music.

And it's not just me; we all do. One morning at breakfast, Phil was laying the table when he suddenly started banging cutlery rhythmically against his knee.

'What are you doing that for?' asked our daughter.

'I'm playing the spoons.'

'You can't play the spoons,' I said.

'This is me: doing it. I've got spoons in my hand and I'm playing them.'

'I've known you for over twenty years,' I said. 'I think I'd know if you could play the spoons.'

He didn't answer at first. He was getting into the swing of it, eyes half closed, knee bouncing up and down.

At last he said jerkily, in time to the music in his head and the pounding of metal on trouser, 'I grew up on a South London council estate. How could I *not* play the spoons?'

It wasn't the dazzling virtuosity I remembered from my youth, but it was a rhythm ... of sorts.

'But ... you're just banging them,' our daughter said with an air of bewilderment. 'Anyone can do that.'

'That's the point,' Phil explained. 'It's music for the masses.' And to prove this, he began to sing along.

'Any old iron, any old iron, any, any, any old iron ...'

I joined in – a harmony of course. And the children, now old enough to have learned self-consciousness themselves, rolled their eyes all over again.

A broken heart

Michael was late. Annoyingly late. Keeping-everybody-waiting-like-we-didn't-have-anything-better-to-do late. When he finally breezed in, he said, 'I'm SO sorry,' with the insouciance of a good-looking young man who knew he could get away with anything. And sure enough, we all pretended we hadn't noticed. He'd gambled on none of us being vulgar enough to tell him off, and damn it, it had worked. Inwardly, though, I was fuming, and the fact that I couldn't say I was fuming made me fume even more.

It was the first time I'd been asked to direct a student production. I hadn't volunteered for it, being very much a limelight kind of a girl. But this was a straightforward revue, sketches and songs we'd performed a hundred times. All it needed was knocking into shape, and then we could take it around that summer's college balls for a few quid a head and as much cheap fizz as we could stomach. Simple. Except that, in a moment of characteristic ditziness – we were all students, after all – the Secretary of the Oxford Revue committee had mistakenly asked Michael to direct the same show. And since neither of us wanted to oust the other, and neither of us quite trusted the other to do it well enough, we'd found ourselves yoked together as co-directors. Four people in the cast and two of us giving notes; it was never going to be easy. But it was about to get unexpectedly harder.

'It's just that while I was cycling here I passed a field of wild poppies,' Michael began.

'Right,' I said, trying to move things along.

'And I remembered you telling me you loved poppies.'

'Right,' I said again, starting to feel uncomfortable.

And with a boyish grin, he produced a slightly crushed wild poppy from the pocket of his jeans and handed it to me, right there in front of everyone. There was an awkward pause. I've never been entirely easy with romantic gestures anyway, and the gear change from quietly aggrieved to pleasantly surprised wasn't a smooth one. During the pause somebody said 'aaah' and I glared at them. Then I took the poppy, and thanked Michael for thinking of me, in a way that was meant to imply that I'd rather he'd just turned up on time. I was also going for a top-note of polite discouragement, but in that I clearly failed. He continued to give me what P G Wodehouse called 'soupy looks' for the two hours of rehearsal that remained.

I should have been delighted. Michael was every bit as handsome as he believed himself to be and rather sweet into the bargain, and at the age of twenty my romantic history had been seriously undistinguished. For one thing, I wasn't especially pretty. I wasn't especially ugly either, just sort of middling. Big eyes, square face, wayward hair – perfectly fine, but not the sort of looks that turn boys' heads. They want leggy girls with self-confidence. Girls who will laugh at their jokes rather than trying to race them to the punchline. Girls who twiddle their hair in an artless, carefree way, not nervously and obsessively like I twiddled mine.

In some ways, I was surprised that boys weren't interested. In the sort of books I liked to read at the time (Jane Austen, George Eliot, the Brontës) passionate men can't get enough of socially awkward, nerdy, shy girls. They're falling over themselves to unlace their inhibitions and show them the polite society version of 'a good time'. But of course those books were *written* by socially awkward, nerdy, shy girls, who arguably turned to writing in the first place to fill the gap in their schedules where 'a good time' was meant to be. It took me longer than it should have done to work that out.

Throughout my teenage years I took a notebook with me to discos, quietly certain that some poetic kindred spirit would come and ask me what I was writing in it. And I'm sure he would have done, had he not been dancing to 'Oops, Upside Your Head' with some girl with flicky hair.

So by the time I went to university, I'd only had a couple of dates, and they'd all been non-starters. There was Dan, who took me out for a pizza, discovered he was allergic to cheese and broke his tooth on an olive pip. There was a catastrophic afternoon in a cinema with Matt, who made me sit though an interminable sci-fi film and kissed me without first removing his chewing gum. And there was Howie, with whom I went out by mistake. I'd been trying to flirt with another boy altogether, using a technique I'd seen in a film whereby you ignore the person you fancy and pretend to be fascinated by his friend. It was a terrible idea, and I really don't recommend it. The boy I was 'ignoring' wasn't interested enough to notice he was being ignored, and poor hapless Howie was quite intoxicated by the attention. Only one other woman had ever hung so rapturously on his every word, and that was his mother. He asked me out to a kosher restaurant the very next weekend and I didn't have the heart to say no. Actually, the date with Howie turned out to be the least worst of the bunch. He was sweet-natured and so innately uncool that he didn't even bother to try, which made him rather relaxing company. And the lokshen pudding was a bonus.

But having got to the age of eighteen without a hint of an actual relationship, and with three years at a women's college ahead of me, I entered Oxford – to put it bluntly – gagging for a boyfriend. I had a sort of shopping list in mind. Ideally I wanted someone with floppy hair and a double-barrelled name – *Brideshead Revisited* was on TV at the time, and I pictured myself sipping Brandy Alexanders in his stately home, while he charmingly patronised the servants. Failing that, I'd have settled for a moody jazz pianist who drank Jack Daniels straight from the bottle, or a sardonic New Yorker. I was pretty open-minded really. On my first weekend, I went to a freshers' disco (throwing caution to the wind, I left my notebook behind) and was asked to dance by a marvellously posh Old Wykehamist. He had the desired double-barrelled name, and though his hair was not so much Sebastian Flyte as 'just got off a long-haul flight', I felt he had potential. After we'd been dancing for a while, he suddenly chuckled to himself and murmured, 'If my dad could see me now ...' I asked him what he meant, and his explanation startled me. 'Dancing with a Jewess,' he said, and it turned out I wasn't an object of desire at all, just a bizarre act of rebellion against some anti-Semitic old bastard.

Then at the end of my first year, I met Ben. Ben was tall, skinny and bespectacled. He made me laugh, and he was very bright. I knew that anyway, but every so often he liked to remind me of it by correcting my grammar. He was intellectually competitive in a way that I hadn't encountered before, so it took a while for this to tip over from quirky and exciting to boorish and irritating. I couldn't understand it: I was going out with him, so clearly I was a big fan. And yet he couldn't contain the urge to impress me. On one occasion over the summer holidays, he'd managed to complete *The Times* crossword on the long train journey down to my home. He was so pleased with himself that he couldn't resist filling in the answers on my mother's copy too. But he didn't own up to her that he'd done it once already and it had taken him four hours; he just sat in front of us both, scrawling the answers, speedily and without apparent effort as if possessed by some strange clue-solving superpower – Crypticite, I suppose it would be called. I think I was meant to be dazzled, but actually I just felt a little disappointed.

It was another crossword-related incident that heralded the end of our relationship. We were attempting to complete one together, this time in *his* mother's living room – what a tempestuous, passionate time were having of it, every date another grid to complete – and the answer to 7 down was 'dour'.

'I think that one's "dour",' I said.

'You mean "dower",' corrected Ben.

'I've always pronounced it "dour". Like "door", but a bit more Scottish.'

'Well, you've always pronounced it wrong,' concluded Ben, making a start on 21 across.

It was a correction too far, and I couldn't let it go. Ben got a dictionary. We were both right, as it turned out, but he was so shocked to discover this that when he went to put the book back, he slightly lost his footing and bumped into the door. I know, I know, I should have let it go, but sometimes it's too damned tempting:

'Mind the dower ...' I said. And thus, I became single again.

So with this history of failed excuses for relationships you can see why gorgeous Michael's romantic gesture of running through fields to pluck a wild poppy for me might have appeared to be an encouraging turn of events. But it was too late. I was – or imagined myself to be – in love with Harry.

Harry was the President of the Oxford Revue, the dark blue equivalent of Cambridge's Footlights. He was a year older than me, intelligent, organised, business-like, brusque and no sufferer of fools. He ran this little student theatre group as if it were the RSC, not just doing the artsy stuff like scripts and casting and arranging gigs, but book-keeping and controlling the management structure. He knew what an audit was, for crying out loud, and he wasn't even twenty-one. Harry rarely delegated to anyone; the choice of director for the ball shows was a rare exception, and the fact that his Secretary then cocked it up only made him more convinced that he had to do everything himself. Consequently, he was always under pressure, stressed and short-tempered. He was also small, stocky, decidedly odd-looking and almost wantonly charmless. Naturally I adored him.

For a couple of weeks prior to the poppy incident I'd been sort of going out with him. That 'sort of' is key to what happened next, so I ought to explain what it meant. Essentially, this being Harry, I'd been the subject of a takeover: not a hostile one, by any means, as I was only too keen on the prospect. But to put it in Harry's terms, the contracts had been drawn up, and the actual merger was pending. First, he had to deal with a period of due diligence – his final exams – which is why Michael and I were drafted in to replace him as directors for the ball season. The last of these shows was the jewel in the crown, Christ Church ball. It was to be just after the end of Harry's finals, so we'd agreed that he'd come along as my guest. It would be our first proper date.

Given that we were all English students, the tangled scenario that night was fittingly Shakespearean. The flawless Michael mooned around after me, like Demetrius chasing Helena, and like her I'd simply never had that effect on such a good-looking bloke before so I assumed it must be a cruel joke. Mainly, though, I was busy trying to look cool around Harry. I wondered when exactly this was going to turn into a date. He'd barely spoken to me since we'd first met up, when seeing me resplendent in my ball gown, his only comment had been: 'Big dress.' You'd have had to be an idiot not to spot that something was wrong, but since in romantic matters, I was that idiot, I didn't. Not, at least, until Piano Paul started making smart-arse remarks.

Piano Paul was the accompanist for the revue. He didn't like me much, and somewhere along the line I'd given up worrying about it or trying to put things right. Most of the time, we maintained a slightly uneasy, gossipy rapport. But from the beginning of that evening it was clear that Paul's latest gossip, the references to which he was keeping maddeningly oblique, was something to do with me. I assumed Harry must have told him we were 'going out'. After all, I'd promised to keep it a secret too, and most of my friends had known for weeks. But whatever he was hinting at, Harry was clearly discomfited by it.

There was another actress in the revue, a girl called Sioned who was a little older than me and studying for a doctorate. There were only two years between us, but Sioned somehow seemed like a grown-up. She had a quality that I couldn't quite put my finger on, but which I now think was probably wisdom. She could see beyond all the petty quarrels and crushes to the bigger picture. I didn't know her very well, but I found her presence oddly comforting; I sensed that some of her maturity might rub off.

We performed our set and Harry stood at the back and watched, but he didn't seem to enjoy it much. And afterwards, he just disappeared. Paul resumed the maddening comments, but he wouldn't be drawn on what he actually knew, and thinking I must have upset Harry in some way, I decided to go looking for him. It was pretty late, and everyone I came across was drunk. I stumbled around the college with increasing desperation, bumping into snogging couples, dodging pools of vomit, and clambering over comatose future cabinet ministers. I asked a few people if they'd seen him, but you couldn't get any sense out of anyone.

It felt like I'd wandered into a grotesque parody of Oxford – all Gothic architecture and decadence and repressed desire. And suddenly, Sioned appeared, handed me a plastic tumbler of wine and bundled me into a quiet room for a talking-to.

'Right,' she began. 'I'm not having this. There's something you need to know, and I'd rather you heard it from me than from Paul or anyone else. Harry is seeing someone. I don't know who she is, and I don't know why he agreed to come here with you rather than just telling you about it, but it's better that you know.' She was right of course. It was infinitely better that I knew. But it sure as hell didn't feel that way.

I spent the last week of term surrounded by my closest friends, a group which now included Sioned. I had officially had my heart broken, and there was, it appeared, a protocol to be followed, which included tea drinking, listening to Billie Holliday records and laughing hysterically at not very much. Harry was nowhere to be seen, and even when I did bump into him for the first time weeks later, nothing at all was mentioned. After 'sort of' going out together, we'd 'sort of' broken up, and without any of the fun stuff in between.

Eleven years later, I was engaged to Phil and appearing in a West End show. One Saturday, in the gap between the matinee and evening performances, I was heading out of the stage door to go and get a sandwich. There was Harry.

'Wow,' I said.

'Should I go away?'

'No, it's fine. Just ... wow.'

He'd come to apologise. After eleven years. I thought that was pretty amazing of him really. And as Phil pointed out when I told him, there's nothing like being engaged and in a successful West End show to make you happy to see the guy who broke your heart. But I didn't need to gloat. Harry just told me what had happened and why he'd behaved the way he had, and it was fine. I forgave him. Of course I did. We were kids, and I – who had been so hopeless in my dealings with the opposite sex – could hardly criticise him for being the same. I forgave him unconditionally, and I really hope he knew that, because the next time I heard about him was when I read his obituary.

To say I couldn't believe it is a cliché, of course. It's always unfathomable when a young person dies, but somehow it was even harder to take in because Harry seemed so grounded, so mature, so in control. Emotionally, as he admitted to me all those years later, he hadn't been any of those things, but he had the air of someone who had sprung from the womb fully formed. I couldn't imagine him being a child, and I couldn't imagine him being old. He was Harry, essence of Harry, ask Harry, Harry will sort it out, Harry will cope. It was that, I realised, that had attracted me to him – I was bumbling around, pretending to understand the world, and he seemed to be the man with the answers. I'd been drawn to Sioned for exactly the same reason. As I launched myself on the ocean of life, I'd been looking around for anchors.

I read the obituary several times, to make sure I hadn't got it wrong, that it really was Harry. He'd got married and had a son, and while I was desperately sad for them that they'd lost him, I was glad for him that he'd found a happy ending. But why was he dead? Cancer, I assumed, or a car crash. But it was neither. It was a cardiac problem he had always carried around with him, unknowingly. It had been there all that time, on a slow-burning fuse: when he was running our shows in Edinburgh, and editing scripts; when he was rehearsing us and getting stressed and laughing and solving everyone's problems; when he was 'sort of' going out with me, and when he was running away. All that time I'd imagined my heart to be broken, and it turns out Harry's really was.

Tennyson in a shed

So who was I going to be? This seemed to me the most pressing question in the first few weeks of university. I needed a 'thing', an image, something to set me apart, to get me noticed, to help me make my mark. I hadn't really thought about it before I went up. I knew who I was at school: I was the hardworking girl who also did plays, the one who was rubbish at sport, but always made fun of herself about it so nobody else had to. But lack of sporting prowess didn't matter any more, and one look at the reading list told me we were all going to be hardworking. I couldn't be the Clever One. Not at Oxford. I'd be lucky not to be the Stupid One. And the queues at every audition meant that it wouldn't be easy being the Acting, Dancing or Singing One either.

For one fleeting moment, I thought I might have stumbled into being the Social One, when a mysterious invitation arrived in the inter-college mail. 'Come for tea with me and Sam, 4pm Thursday. Bring a bottle. We're not having tea!! Toby xx' it read. I spent a happy morning wondering who Toby and Sam were, and how I had unexpectedly attracted their attention.

Then I began to wonder how I was going to join them for 'tea' if I didn't actually know what college they were at, and it was as I scoured the envelope more closely for clues that I noticed the invitation was actually for Rebecca Fane in the year above me. She, plainly, was the One Having All the Fun.

As the weeks went by, I became increasingly conscious of the girls who had their 'thing'. There was Imogen, who dressed entirely in Edwardian clothes – all pleated shoulders, stiff collars and hobble skirts; Fi the somewhat anachronistic hippy chick who'd spent her year off living in a squat and was permanently shrouded in a cloud of patchouli; and Laura, the rower, who got up earlier than any student in the history of further education, and spoke about strokes and catching crabs and finding the right-sized cox without even a nod towards irony.

I made a couple of feeble attempts. I dressed in nothing but red and black for a week or so, but nobody noticed. I wore my dressing gown to a party, claiming it was a smoking jacket, but I just felt a fool, and anyway, I didn't smoke.

By now I had befriended Jane, and she already had her 'thing'. She was a radical thinker. While I was here to dip my toe into the literary establishment, Jane had already decided to rebel against it. She'd chosen this college because here she could be taught – not by some plodding historical or biographical theorist, but by Tess Wakefield. It was a name that held no further resonance for me than that I'd seen it in the prospectus. But for Jane, Tess was going to be her guide into a process of thought that would dominate the rest of her life. And so infectious was her excitement that I decided to follow her lead. It would be easy for me to turn my back on traditional literary criticism, since I'd never read any in the first place. All I had to do was to ask for Tess as my tutor, and I too could be part of a revolution. And yes, it was, strictly speaking, Jane's 'thing' and not mine. But hey, it was better than the dressing gown.

The one fact everyone knew about Tess was that she held her tutorials in a shed. Nowadays, when so many people have offices in their gardens, this doesn't sound strange. But it did back in the Eighties, not least because this was a university, and if there was one thing you wouldn't expect a university to be short of, it was rooms to hold tutorials in. If Tess was teaching in a shed it had to be for one of two reasons: either she didn't want to be linked to the college, or they didn't want to be linked to her. It never occurred to us that she might just prefer to work at home. She had teenage sons and several cats, and now that I'm a grown-up, I can see that the shed arrangement meant she could rustle up dinner between tutorials and get the washing on the line. But before we knew about such things, we believed there was some mystery about the shed, and no one was going to persuade us otherwise.

She specialised in post-structuralist theory, and though I didn't have the first clue what that might mean, it was clear to me within minutes of arriving in her shed that, academically, we weren't in Kansas any more.

Tess was a tall, handsome woman with short dark hair and a perpetually furrowed brow. She always wore several layers of woollies, because the shed was – well, a shed. It had no insulation, a felt roof and only a bar fire for heating. There were books everywhere of course, on the shelves, on the floor, all over the sofa, chairs and desk. You couldn't sit or move your feet or put your coffee cup down without having to shift one mound of books and balance them on top of another. It was wonderful – a thinker's grotto. But it was also an intimidating place to read aloud your eight closely written A4 sides of essay. You sensed the eyes of a thousand authors and critics rolling in disdain.

To say the shed was smoky would be an understatement. The rugs, curtains, upholstery, even the wooden walls themselves had been cured by Tess's French cigarettes. You could have taken in a fillet of raw salmon at the beginning of a tutorial and eaten it on a bagel by the time you left. God knows how many cigarettes she got through every day, but no sooner had she stubbed one out than she'd light the next. And yet, she never seemed to have matches or a lighter. Instead, while she listened to you reading your work, she'd tear off a bit of paper from the *Guardian* or maybe, for all I knew, a previous student's essay. She'd twist it into a point and jab the end against one of the bars of her electric fire. As she withdrew it, little sparks would spiral downwards towards the flammable piles of books. Occasionally she'd stamp one out with her foot, but usually she'd ignore them and concentrate on holding the flaming spill against the end of her Gauloise. Once it was lit, she'd stub out the twist of paper in an ashtray on the floor, sending more sparks flying around and settling on the rug. Every time I went to the shed, I was faintly surprised that it and Tess weren't just a smouldering pile of cinders.

In my first week, I read her my thoughts on Tennyson. She wasn't impressed. She didn't even pretend to be; in fact I'm pretty sure that before I'd finished analysing the first few stanzas of 'Maud', she was planning what to make her boys for tea. She sent me off with a list of books she wanted me to read before making her sit through any more of this crap, though she didn't put it quite as bluntly as that. Top of this list was a book by the American academic Harold Bloom. I bought it on my way back to college and read the first two chapters that night. It was a revelation to me – though not quite in the way I think Tess had imagined.

Throughout my schooldays – which had only just ended of course – I'd known what to expect from a textbook. If it was about biology, it would be a struggle – there'd be terms I didn't understand, concepts that were quite beyond me, whole chapters that I simply couldn't grasp. English, though, was my subject. I *got* English. Sure, it was a challenge to interpret certain works, but I understood the basics, I had a strong foundation, I'd get there in the end. The Bloom book, though, seemed to me to be a biology textbook – about English. It was full of words that I recognised, but that clearly didn't mean what I'd always thought they did. I felt the ground shifting beneath my feet, and it was horrible. I asked Jane to help, because she could speak post-structuralist. She taught me some basic vocabulary and the rudiments of grammar. I was a long way from fluent, but I probably had enough phrases to, say, order a structuralist meal and complain that there was phenomenology in my soup. Crucially I got through Tess's next tutorial.

From then on, she tolerated me. I won't say she liked me, or ever had any feelings for me warmer than pity, but she put up with me. Apparently, the Bloom book was something of a test. Some people took one look and asked to be assigned another tutor. Others, like Jane, relished the chance to think in a whole new way. But most of us just had a stab at it, allowing its contents to slip in and out of focus as we read. Sometimes I understood a section, or at least I thought I did. I'd run it past Jane first, and if she didn't wince and look troubled, then I'd feel confident enough to put it in an essay. And from time to time, I'd write something that Tess was pleased with. You knew when she approved, because she'd raise her eyebrows, nod her head slowly and say, 'Ya, ok. Fine.' And it would feel like you were close to the summit of Everest, whereas in reality you were seeing it on a postcard.

Looking back on it, I think the shed was more than just a practical arrangement for a working mum. I think it was hugely significant. Tess wasn't part of the establishment, and she wanted you to know it. She was a maverick. If they'd ever made a series about an English don who also solved crimes, they would have modelled it on her. She had it all: the brooding expression, the uncompromising attitude, the curl of cigarette smoke rising from her fingers. They'd call her into the office and say, 'Tess, there's a poem here. It's about some dame from Shalott.' And she'd break into a wry half-smile, and say, 'I think we both know that's not what it's about at all.'

The shed was what set Tess apart from the other poor saps. It was her version of Columbo's raincoat or Kojak's lollipop or Morse's classical records: a maverick's badge of identity. It told you straight off the bat that to be taught by her, you had to go the extra mile. You had to leave behind you the comfort of the college and the lazy thought patterns of school. You had to venture into the unknown.

I'd love to reveal that I cracked the code and became a star student. But I didn't. The truth is, I never really grasped post-structuralism. There were moments when I saw the beauty of it; when I looked at a text in a whole new way, and found ideas and themes within it that I'd never even dreamed of. But more often than not, I was reading from a script – keeping to myself what I felt the poem really meant, or at least what it really meant to me, and giving Tess the interpretation that I thought she wanted to hear. She knew that, of course. There was no pulling the wool over her eyes; she knew a fake when she saw one. But I think she was quite touched that I was even playing the part of someone who understood. It was a costume I'd adopted, like Isobel with her Edwardian clothes.

Jane was an explorer – born to journey into uncharted intellectual waters. Me? I was a gap-year traveller, taking a few photos and bragging to my friends about the experience. It wasn't my 'thing' any more than rowing would have been, and I wasn't impressing anyone, least of all Tess. After I'd been with her for a couple of terms, I wrote an essay on Browning, which had been a particularly torturous effort for me, and she sent me notes on it that were meant for another student. I politely complained, and she seemed both aggrieved and utterly mystified. It turned out, she genuinely didn't know which one of us was which.

But that in itself is one of the most important aspects of university: learning what *isn't* your 'thing'; finding out that there's more to being special than having a gimmick. The shed was a physical reminder that there were areas of academia that were open to me if I really wanted to work hard. But I didn't quite fit in. It was partly that I wasn't a great thinker, but also that I didn't take it seriously enough. I couldn't resist mocking it a little, laughing at the intensity of it all, going for the joke. When I got a smile out of Jane by suggesting, as a title for her essay on linguistic theory, 'I Used to Be a Semiotician, but Now I'm Not Saussure', I realised, at last, that maybe making laboured jokes was my 'thing'. I became the Comedy one.

But in the meantime, for one hour every week, I'd walk a mile to sit in a fug of carcinogens, stifled by the sense of my own inadequacy. I'd read aloud the essay I'd stayed up all night writing. And Tess would smoke and stare out of the window.

For a few exciting weeks, I imagined she was thinking, 'Well, that idea was muddled, the final paragraph was just plain vapid, but one of those thoughts had promise, so ya. OK. Fine.'

But probably, she was gazing at the clouds, willing me to read faster, so that she could gather in the washing before it rained.

Normal

I was sitting on a bus one day when a woman came down the stairs holding a rabbit on a lead. The rabbit was sizeable (I might as well say 'fat' since there's not much chance of it reading this), wearing a pink lead and had a pink bow in its fur. Its owner was young and soberly dressed, and on a scale of eccentricity she'd definitely be nearer the end marked 'rum cove' than the one marked 'best avoided'. Nonetheless, as she staggered downstairs with it, all the other passengers decided she was probably a dangerous oddball. You could tell this because they turned their backs and pretended she wasn't there.

Yet apart from the fact that the rabbit wasn't a dog, there was nothing odd in her behaviour at all. She stood an acceptable distance from her nearest fellow passengers, hung on sensibly to the rail with the hand that wasn't clutching her pet, and behaved in all respects like a woman carrying a shopping bag, rather than a camped-up, over-sized bunny. And it was this very normality, I realised, that marked her out as strange. Had she been grinning or catching people's eye, or even wearing something quirky; had she, in short, been self-conscious about holding a rabbit on a bus, people would have branded her a perfectly harmless attention-seeker and thought no more about it. But no. Here was someone self-confident enough to do something borderline weird and make no apology for it whatsoever.

It happened that just moments before boarding the bus I, the anonymous-looking woman on the back seat holding nothing stranger than my handbag, had done something far odder; something that, even to my mind, defied logic.

We were having friends for dinner that night and I'd decided to make a pudding that required a large quantity of white chocolate buttons. Nursery food was popular at the time, and I was confident my friends would appreciate the amusing bathos of a posh-looking dessert made out of sweets. If nothing else, they were bound to be impressed by my casual use of the term 'amusing bathos'.

Now, I'm the sort of person who is so preoccupied with appearing normal that I can't buy four bottles of wine without remarking in a jaunty voice that they're not all for me. As I stood at the checkout with a couple of dozen mini bags of white chocolate buttons, I was already formulating apologies about how the Milky Bar Kid was coming to stay. I wasn't sure the assistant was old enough to get that reference though, so I started tossing a few other ideas around but kept running headlong towards punchlines about diabetes and, looking at the queue, I knew I'd be playing it to the wrong crowd. It crossed my mind to say nothing, but that was impossible. I was buying twenty-four bags of chocolate buttons. It was simply beyond me not to explain it.

When it was my turn, I piled the bags of sweets on to the conveyor belt and smiled a friendly don't-judge-me kind of smile. The assistant smiled back in a way that suggested she already had, so I now felt compelled to speak.

'Kid's birthday party,' I said, rolling my eyes as if to say, 'We've all been there, right?'

It was a lie, an outright lie, and an unprompted one at that. But somehow, to my skewed brain, it made me seem more normal.

The assistant politely asked whether it was for a girl or a boy.

'My daughter,' I lied again, but as I did so I realised that since the supermarket was near my daughter's school, and her real birthday party had only been only a month before, it was just possible that somebody within earshot would know that wasn't true. I now had to qualify my pointless lie with another far more serious one.

'My younger daughter,' I said. My voice was sounding less confident now. The chances of somebody knowing the date of my daughter's birthday were remote, but even a casual playground acquaintance would know I didn't have a younger child.

'How old?' asked the assistant indulgently. I panicked. How old would a child have to be for chocolate buttons to be suitable party food?

'She's three,' I said, and then in a panicky tone, 'FOUR … no, THREE.'

My large order of chocolate buttons had aroused no suspicion, but this uncertainty looked distinctly dodgy. And it was. In order to appear normal I had just invented a third child for myself. It was quite the maddest thing I could have done.

So, on the bus, a short time later, I looked in admiration at the bunny woman for having the self-possession not to call out, 'Look at me carrying a rabbit on a lead! I'm doing it as a bet ... to raise money for charity. I'm not bonkers!' The other passengers were not so impressed though. They continued to look the other way, occasionally sneaking glances at the woman with the rabbit and smirking as if to say, 'You couldn't make it up!'

Another woman came down the stairs of the bus, spotted the rabbit, cooed a few niceties at its owner and stroked its foot – the rabbit's, not the owner's. The latter was pleased, I think, not just that someone was admiring her pet, but that she was in some way being brought in from the cold. She smiled, and I did too, feeling relieved that the awkward tension had been broken. For a glorious moment, the bus had become a warmer, more tolerant place.

But then an odd thing happened. The second woman, though she'd stopped petting the rabbit, continued to stare at it – a stare that went on far, far too long. The bus stopped and still she stared. It started again, and still she carried on peering at the rabbit, yet not engaging with its owner. Slowly, the balance of normality shifted. The owner, who'd worn her little eccentricity with such pride, began to look uneasy as this seemingly 'normal' woman gazed freakishly at her rabbit. Did she want to steal it? Was she planning to cook it? Her body tensed, her face hardened and finally she did what all the other passengers had done to her: she turned her back and pretended the woman wasn't there.

I have a friend who describes nearly everyone she meets as 'weird'. For a long time, I used to think that maybe I'd missed some significant fact about them, because to me they seemed quite ordinary. But what she means by 'weird' is 'different from me'. In a way, I quite like that blanket acknowledgement of difference – it normalises the abnormal. My friend has created a level playing field on which those with neuroses are no odder than those with picky eating habits – they're all weird.

For all my obsessive attempts to appear normal at first glance, in a supermarket queue or on a bus, I'm quite happy for people to know I'm weird. After that failed effort to appear normal to the woman behind the checkout, for instance, here I am gleefully retelling how abnormally I behaved. I suppose it's about wanting to control people's perception of me: I want them to think I'm normal, and only then can I reveal how not normal I am.

Some years ago, I tweeted a reference to having panic attacks, and subsequently found myself described by journalists as 'bravely speaking out about my mental health issues'. But the truth is, I don't think I have a mental health issue. To me, being anxious is perfectly normal. OK, panic attacks are a little extreme even for me, but I don't see why it's brave to write about them. Bravery suggests it's something I should be ashamed of, and I'm not. It's a pain in the arse to be anxious, it's a massive pain in the arse to have a panic attack, but it's not embarrassing. And I'm someone who finds buying chocolate buttons embarrassing. I'm not embarrassed about being neurotic because I don't think I know a single person who would properly qualify as 'normal'.

I tend to think of mental health in much the same way as physical health. As far as I'm aware, there's no such thing as a perfect, flawless body. Even if you're super-fit, you might get back problems or headaches; you could have weak knees or fallen arches or spots at exactly the same time as you have movie-star good looks. If you also develop heart trouble or cancer or diabetes – OK, you've got a problem, and you'd better get it seen to. The same is true of mental health: you may seem like the most well-adjusted, confident, successful person on the planet, but that doesn't mean you won't get depressed sometimes or be terrified of heights. If your mood swings or anxiety get so bad that you can no longer function though, or if you're losing touch with reality, or starting to be a danger to yourself or other people – yep, that's serious, and you definitely need some help. What I don't quite get is why those problems are considered embarrassing when cancer and heart trouble are not. It may be because mental illness is harder to diagnose, that there are wide parameters, so it's awkward knowing at what point you can say, with certainty, 'That's depression all right, sure as eggs are eggs.' But I think it's more complicated than that. I think it's to do with our atavistic fear of madness.

When I was a child, everyone knew the name of their local asylum. You knew it because it was constantly invoked as the worst place imaginable, and as the place where you'd be 'carted off to' if you didn't conform. One of the most common synonyms for chaos, bedlam, comes from Bethlem, the name of an asylum. I once visited an old-fashioned 'mental hospital' shortly before it was closed down. There were long, dark corridors stretching into infinity, bars on the windows, which were anyway too high up to see out of, people shouting and groaning randomly. It was terrifying, and if you weren't mad when you arrived there, you would be pretty soon afterwards. I'd gone there with a singing group to perform an evening of music hall songs. Those poor patients – just when they thought things couldn't get any worse, four do-gooding teenagers turned up to 'ta-ra-ra-boom-dee-ay' the hell out of them. I'll never forget the horror of that place, and I was only there for an hour or so.

Given that all of us have a constant stream of curious, disconnected and sometimes distressing thoughts running through our brains, and that it's hard to know when those thoughts are just harmless electrical firings and when they've tipped over into something more disturbing; and given that for centuries if you went and asked for help, there was a fighting chance they'd lock you away in some hideous earth-bound hell, you can start to see why people have tended not to want to talk about what's going through their minds. In the old days, we knew that lumbago was common, because people happily complained about it to anyone who'd listen, but nobody told you they had panic attacks or depression or social phobia. You kept it to yourself, neatly bottled up, where it would fester and ferment and get a whole lot worse.

We're getting used to the idea that lots of us have little neuroses, and for that we can thank Sigmund Freud if we want to, but mainly it's down to American movies and TV series, which make seeing a shrink seem like the new normal. In Britain, we still have a slightly sniffy disdain for people who go into therapy – we tend to think it's self-indulgent, that they should just pull themselves together – but we're slowly starting to see that difference isn't necessarily weird, in fact difference isn't necessarily different. People are opening up about having break-downs and living with depression or anxiety. I read something recently saying that so many celebrities were 'coming out' about their problems, it was almost becoming fashionable, this year's must-have accessory – a Prada bag and a phobia. I don't think that's right though. For something to be chic, it also has to be rare and unobtainable – neurosis is neither of those.

Even accepting that there's no such thing as normal, that everybody you pass in the street and sit next to on public transport is every bit as peculiar as you are, society depends on a set of conventions by which the majority can abide. If your peculiarity rolls smoothly alongside everybody else's, you can live quite equably with others. But if it bumps up against too many people or flies in the face of decorum, you can inadvertently make things pretty uncomfortable. I'm all for taking the stigma away from mental health problems, but I'd be lying if I said I'd never given someone a wide berth because they seemed a wee bit, well, odd. If you're going to embrace people's right to walk through life in their own unique world, you also have to embrace everybody else's right not to want to get drawn into it.

Many years ago, I was working in central London and had nipped out for a breath of air at lunchtime. Walking down one of the busiest shopping streets in the capital, I slowly became aware that I was being followed. I don't know what suddenly alerted me to it, but in that way that we are all subconsciously checking out our environment all the time, I started to wonder why a particular woman had been walking quite so closely behind me for the last ten minutes. Because I wasn't sure, and because it seemed like I was just being, well, neurotic, I stopped to look in a shop window, assuming that she'd pass me. She didn't. She stopped too. Only, she didn't look in the window, she looked at me looking in the window. I glanced at her, thinking she'd look away. But, like the woman on the bus staring at the rabbit, she just went right on peering at me. I repeated this action outside several further shops, and every time she did the same thing. There was no doubt about it. For some unfathomable reason – perhaps in a cloudy part of her psyche I reminded her of someone, or she just thought I needed keeping an eye on – she was following my every move and she clearly wasn't going to stop.

I was only half a mile away from where I worked, but something told me that it wouldn't be a good idea to lead her there. After all, I might be able to shake her off for now, but she'd know where I was going to be later and the next day and for some time after that. In broad daylight, in the middle of Covent Garden, I suddenly felt very afraid.

I went into a shop, a tiny little one-roomed outlet for tights and scarves. There was no chance of losing her in here, but I hoped she might just get bored and forget about me. I casually browsed the shelves, picking up multi-packs of pop socks and reading the washing instructions in exhaustive detail, but every time I peeped out of the window, she was there. Eventually, I knew I was going to have to ask for help.

'Excuse me,' I said to the young assistant, 'I know this sounds a bit bizarre, but you see that woman out there? Well, I don't know why, but she's following me.'

The girl behind the counter looked outside. Then she looked at me again with barely concealed disbelief that *anyone* would want to follow *me*.

'Who is she?' she asked.

'I don't know. That's the point. She's just been walking behind me for ages.'

'It's busy, though. I mean there were probably a lot of people walking behind you,' she said, as if to a dim-witted child.

'Yes, I know that. But look at her. She's just standing there staring at me. They're not all doing that, are they?'

'Well, I can't really get involved, I'm afraid,' she said.

'No,' I explained, 'I don't want you to sort her out or anything. I just thought perhaps if I disappeared, she might forget about me and move on.'

I realised as soon as I'd uttered it that 'disappeared' was an unfortunate choice of word. With its connotations of witchcraft, I'd implied that I wanted some sort of spell performed. Weighing up the two participants in this strange narrative – the passive woman quietly staring at the window and the agitated one saying she wanted to disappear – she had clearly decided I was the oddball.

'Do you have a back exit, or another room I could just hide in for a bit? Then you could tell me when she's gone, and I'll be on my way. And if she doesn't go, maybe we could call the police.'

'I can't let you in the stockroom,' she said. 'No disrespect, but you might nick stuff.'

'Yes, I can see that. But I don't know what else to do. I'm desperate. I'll happily let you check my bag when I come out.'

She thought for a minute, and then glancing out of the window and seeing the woman still standing there looking unblinkingly in my direction, she gave me the benefit of the doubt.

She showed me into the stockroom and shut the door. It was small and dark in there, and the only window was barred. It was exactly the sort of room that would usually trigger my claustrophobia, but today I had bigger fish to fry. I pushed that to the back of my mind and waited. The walls were lined with shelves, packed with boxes of hosiery. It occurred to me that it was to all intents and purposes a padded cell. What if I'd imagined the whole thing? What if she hadn't been following me? I'd nipped out for a coffee and ended up doubting my sanity. Maybe a padded cell was just where I belonged.

After a brief hiatus, the door opened and the shop assistant poked her head in.

'She's gone.'

'Thank you so much,' I said. And I waved my open bag at her to prove I hadn't stolen any slipper socks.

I came out into the daylight of the shop and peered down the road – my pursuer was nowhere to be seen. I felt a surge of relief. There was a customer in the shop now, but I thanked the assistant profusely again, and stepped outside. As I turned to shut the door behind me, I was just in time to catch her gesturing in my direction and mouthing a single word to the customer: 'Weird.'

Slumming it

In our final year at university, a group of friends and I decided to live out of college. It was the accepted pattern that students would stay in college halls for their first two years, to acclimatise to being away from home and allow them to focus on their work. But most people used the third year as a chance to stand on their own two feet. I was twenty-one, for goodness sake. In another life, I could have been fighting a war or married with kids or running a business by now. It was high time I grew up. A bit.

There were four of us in the household: Jane, Lou and me from one college, and a bloke called Steve, whom none of us knew. He had answered our ad on the risky assumption that sharing with three women might prove to be a more civilised affair than sharing with three other men. As it happened Steve struck gold because all of us were easygoing, moderately tidy and pretty good at cooking, and we struck gold because we had a lovely, wry, amiable bloke around the place. We were also, every one of us, as guileless and naïve as baby lambs.

We didn't choose our flat – it chose us, as it was the only one we could afford. It consisted of two floors above an empty retail unit that had once sold office equipment. To access our new home, you had to let yourself in through a door at the side, then walk down a dank passage into a courtyard filled with old electrical appliances, bits of scaffolding and other detritus. At the far end was a tumbledown shed, but if you turned back on yourself, a second key would let you enter the rear door. Once inside, you walked up a steep flight of stairs covered, in a threadbare kind of a way, with a frankly hideous carpet. This same carpet ran throughout the flat. There was no escape from it and, it turned out, no way of cleaning it. Things just sort of stuck to the surface: you couldn't remove them and they were never absorbed. They just sat there, bearing witness to the careless act that had created them, until overtaken by some greater stain.

One of the things we had all wanted was a communal area. We had a rosy vision of sitting around in our living room discussing the issues of the day over a glass of wine, and maybe a nibble or two. This place had a living room, but it was so small, and so dominated by the ghastly carpet, an unexplained smell, and a sofa which unquestionably had fleas, that we literally never used it; in fact I barely crossed the threshold more than once, and only then because my boyfriend had parked his bike in it.

Instead, we would congregate in one of the bedrooms or in the heart of the flat – our long, thin kitchen. It was here that we took it in turns to create communal meals with varying degrees of success. Jane was our most adventurous cook, forever making stock from leftover bits and pieces. Where I came from, waste was waste – but to Jane, it was an opportunity. Several times she intercepted me as I was heading for the kitchen bin and commandeered my scraps as a basis for the next night's supper. It was, I now see, very sensible frugality, but at the time I just thought it was a bit weird and told her so. She didn't seem to mind. Jane had a brain more enormous and complex than any I've encountered before or since. Her approach to food matched her approach to her studies: rigorous, unconventional and unfathomably impressive.

Lou was the baker: she made cakes and scones and occasionally bread that was wholesome and earnest and took an age to chew. Lou also sewed, knitted, nurtured her pet hamster and cleaned the flat. She had decided domesticity was her thing and none of us, naturally, wanted to disabuse her of this. She could easily have been created by Beatrix Potter were it not for the fact that she had the filthiest sense of humour of anyone I have ever encountered, and an unparalleled ability to pick up gossip. She'd roll up her sleeves, pound some dough, and tell you everything you wanted to know, and a very great deal that you didn't, about whoever you cared to name.

My cooking was serviceable and hearty – enormous portions of pasta and soup and ratatouille. I was in training to be a Jewish mother – nobody was going to leave my table hungry. And Steve, who, as far as I recall, had never made anything more complicated than a bacon sandwich when he moved in, was determined to give cooking his best shot. One week, he spotted a recipe for garlic soup in a magazine, and decided to have a go. Unfortunately, this being a student flat, the magazine disappeared somewhere under a pile of god knows what, so he had to make it from memory. I still don't know what the vital ingredient he missed out was, but I'm guessing it was the one that would have made it edible. We were all presented with a bowl of warm water with whole, unpeeled garlic cloves floating in it. None of us wanted to be unkind, so we struggled through the first few mouthfuls, adding lavish amounts of salt and pepper, until Steve wondered aloud whether anyone else thought he might have got it slightly wrong.

That alone tells you what our home was like: we loved each other, looked out for each other and treated each other with absolute respect. It couldn't have been a more delightful atmosphere. And as the house itself became increasingly unfit for habitation, the laughter just got more hysterical.

Over the stove was a bare light bulb, and when it rained heavily, water would come through the roof, trickle down the live cable and drip into whatever we were cooking. It's amazing none of us was electrocuted or poisoned or both. Jane raised this with our landlord Mr Wills in a series of increasingly stiffly worded letters. She peppered them with references to Dickens and to Mayhew's *London Labour and the London Poor*, which we all felt were nicely apposite and couldn't fail to hammer the message home. But Mr Wills seemed oddly impervious to her rhetoric and we never got more than an empty promise to sort it out. There was a tiny bathroom on the main floor, and on the downstairs landing, next to the deserted living room, an additional toilet. Shortly after we moved in, Lou saw something in there that was 'at least a mouse and possibly a rat' and from that day onwards, nobody ventured in. But we rarely complained about anything, other than the death-trap kitchen light bulb, because we were trying to be grown-ups. We felt that we had to just get on with things. It was only when my parents brought Grandma Dolly up one weekend that we changed the way we looked at it.

Grandma knew a thing or two about life at the bottom of the ladder, having started out in an East End tenement. So when, after looking round our student flat, she turned to my mother and said in a loud stage whisper, 'Oh my gawd, she's living in a slum,' we finally realised Mr Wills was ripping us off. We thought long and hard about this, talked late into the night about the injustice of preying on people's vulnerability, and debated the best way to make a stand. Finally, we took the decisive action of leaving things as they were and trying not to let it get us down.

Mr Wills – for reasons best known to himself, but which almost certainly included the words 'cheap', 'job lot' and 'man in a pub' – had fitted the flat with a musical doorbell. It had a repertoire of about eight songs, if you could call them songs, all delivered with such ear-splitting tinniness that it sounded like someone was practising the stylophone on your cranium.

One night, shortly after we'd gone to bed, the doorbell rang. I got up, fumbled around for my dressing gown and bumped into Lou in the hall.

'Are you expecting anyone?' I asked.

'No. You?'

'No.'

The doorbell had finished its nasty performance by now and we decided to ignore it and go back to bed. Moments later though, it started again, playing a different tune. And this time, it continued into the next one, and the next. Someone was leaning on it. The others were up by now and we all went into my room, which overlooked the front door, to peer out. In the darkness, we could just about make out the top of someone's head: a man, we thought, with dark curly hair. None of us knew anyone who looked like that. We let the curtain drop and stood in a huddle, whispering to each other.

'Maybe it's Mr Wills.'

'He's bald.'

'And he's got a key.'

'And it's 11.30.'

'Maybe we should call the police.'

'You can't dial 999 because there's someone at the door. It's wasting police time.'

'We could just answer it.'

'NO. You don't open the door to strangers late at night. Do you?'

The truth was none of us had any idea. About anything. We were playing at this 'living alone' thing. Just months before, we'd had a college porter to handle such situations. And before that, our dads. It suddenly felt scary to be a grown-up. If you misjudged a situation like this, you could end up being reconstructed on *Crimewatch*.

Here we were, four children, clever enough to have got into university, but simple enough to be tyrannised by a doorbell.

It was Jane, of course, who thought of the answer. She opened my bedroom window and leaned out.

'Excuse me,' she called, politely.

The curly haired man looked up. We all crowded round her to take a look.

'Do you want something?'

'Is Harvey there?' said the man.

'Harvey? No. Sorry, you've got the wrong address.'

She closed the window. But the man didn't move. We let the curtain drop but carried on peering through the cracks at each side. After a few moments, he rang the doorbell again.

Steve was feeling brave.

'I'll go and talk to him.'

'NO,' we all chorused. 'You might get stabbed … or shot.'

Steve opened the window.

'Excuse me, mate …' he called. Just because someone might want to murder you, there was no need to be impolite.

'Could you stop ringing the doorbell, please? We're trying to get some sleep.'

The curly haired man slowly looked around, then up again. He seemed to be trying to locate Steve's voice, as if he'd forgotten that Jane had called to him from the same window moments before.

'Is Harvey there?' he said again. It was exactly the same inflection as the first time. There was no acknowledgement that we'd already covered this ground – and it made us think that perhaps he wasn't, as my dad would have put it, quite the full shilling.

'There isn't anyone called Harvey here, mate,' said Steve gently. 'You're ringing the wrong doorbell. Do you mind letting us get some sleep now?'

The man looked at him, blankly.

'I'm looking for Harvey.'

'We've drifted into a Beckett play,' Lou whispered, and we told her to be quiet.

'Maybe you can call Harvey,' I suggested, 'and check the address.'

'Harvey doesn't have a phone. That's why I've come round to talk to him.'

'OK,' I said, trying to think of a different way to explain the situation. 'But he doesn't live here, you see. So you can't talk to him. He lives ... somewhere else. Sorry.'

The man looked up at me for a minute, then slowly moved away from the door. We watched as he ambled off down the street. Then we all went into the fetid kitchen, made tea, and congratulated ourselves on clearing another of the hurdles adulthood was putting in our path.

The next night, at around the same time, the doorbell began its endless toll again. He was back, leaning against it, demanding our attention. It went on for ages, but we ignored it and eventually it stopped. But the night after that, it happened again.

By now, we were less scared and more determined to sort it out. All four of us went downstairs, through the passageway and opened the front door. For the first time, we could see more of our visitor than just the top of his head. He was a chubby, short man in his thirties, with a pleasant face. He certainly didn't look like a mass murderer, but then if mass murderers looked like mass murderers, the world would be a simpler and a safer place.

'Is Harvey here?' he asked, as we knew he would.

We took it in turns to explain to him, as patiently as we could, that there was no Harvey and he'd obviously made a mistake. He looked at us calmly, blankly, but showed no sign of understanding or giving up. We told him that we were students, that we all lived together as friends, that we would know if there was anyone else living with us because it wasn't a very big flat. We explained about the musical doorbell and how we all had essays to write and it was disturbing us. We were floundering,

vainly trying to make him understand a little about our lives
and how difficult he was making things, but becoming uncomfortably aware how much *more* difficult his life must have been.
Eventually, when our barrage of useless information stopped,
he opened his mouth to speak. It was slow, as if he was trying
to wade through a lot of muddy thoughts in his head.

'Harvey does live here. I've been here. I've seen him.'

'Maybe it was a long time ago,' suggested Lou. 'Did Harvey
live here before we moved in?'

'I don't know. Did you live here last week?'

'Yes,' said Lou.

'Well so did Harvey.'

We'd reached an impasse. We all looked at him for a while
and he looked right back at us. Eventually, I said 'OK, well
look. Harvey isn't here, so ... I think you're going to have to
go now. I'm sorry to be rude, but ... you know.'

If it's possible to close a door in someone's face politely,
then that's what we did. As we walked back down the passage,
we could still make out the shape of him, distorted through
the frosted glass.

'Maybe we *should* call the police,' I suggested. 'I mean, he
seems kind of vulnerable.'

We walked up the stairs in silence and into the kitchen. I
put the kettle on and Lou opened the cake tin. The doorbell
rang again.

'I wonder if he'd like a scone,' Lou said.

A few moments later we all stood on the doorstep again,
watching him eat one. He'd told us his name was Paul. We
asked him where he lived, and he said the exact address as if
he'd learned it by rote and the only way he could say it was

in one breath. It sounded like it might be a hostel. When he'd finished his scone, he asked if he could see Harvey now.

'He really isn't here, Paul,' Jane said.

'Can I just have a look?' he asked, and there was something so innocent in the way he said it that we stood aside and let him into the passage. I suppose we'd all come to the conclusion that it was the only way to make him understand; and that we outnumbered him, and he seemed rather helpless, and that even if he was dangerous, he was less likely to kill someone who'd given him a homemade scone.

Paul walked straight through the passage and into the courtyard. But he didn't attempt to go through our back door. Instead he crossed the yard and headed for the tumbledown shed. He knocked on the door.

'Harvey. It's me, Paul,' he shouted. And to our amazement, the door opened and he went inside.

It turned out Harvey did live there. He'd been there the whole time, and we'd neither seen him, nor heard him, nor even spotted a light.

We went upstairs to our flat and tried to get our heads around this curious development. It was a shed, nothing more than that. It can't have had running water or plumbing. How could we have been oblivious to another human being living in such close proximity? And if our place was squalid, how much worse must his have been? I got angry. I wanted to write a letter to Mr Wills and ask him what he was doing letting people live in sheds, and not telling us. Better still, I wanted Jane to write it. But she was looking at it from a different angle.

'I don't think Mr Wills knows anything about it,' she said. 'I reckon Harvey's a squatter.'

This put a different complexion on things. We still didn't like the idea of this secretive stranger in our midst, but anyone who could put one over on Mr Wills was worthy of our admiration.

'The fact is,' Steve said thoughtfully, polishing off another of Lou's scones, 'he's been there all this time and he hasn't bothered us. We haven't heard a peep out of him. Really, you couldn't ask for a better neighbour.'

'But it doesn't seem right for *him*,' I said. This whole scenario brought out my suburban side. 'I mean, what must it be like in there? It can't be healthy living like that.'

'But that's his choice,' said Lou. 'It's not really any of our business.'

And I had to concede she was right. There didn't seem to be much we could do about it, and there didn't even seem to be a reason to try.

Harvey stayed living in the shed for the rest of the year. He kept himself entirely to himself. Jane said he once popped in to borrow some milk, like a character from a Seventies sitcom might do, but I never laid eyes on him. I only knew he was there because Paul would visit. Sometimes this didn't happen for weeks or months at a time, and we'd wonder if they'd had a row. It occurred to us too that Harvey might have gone away for a while; that perhaps he was in and out of prison or travelling to find work. We never found out how he'd got a key for the front door, and we never told Mr Wills.

Whatever his circumstances, we lived out the rest of our student days in parallel with him. While we were falling in love and rehearsing plays and cooking meals and studying for our finals, just across the courtyard Harvey was in his shed, struggling through as best he could, with only Paul for company.

A disagreement with Mr Rothko

It was Jane's idea to go to the Rothko exhibition. If she hadn't suggested it, the rare chance to see large numbers of his paintings hung together would have passed me by, and I would always have regretted it. Besides, since she had moved away from London, being with Jane was a rarity too. I wanted to see her and I wanted to see the Rothkos. Just not necessarily at the same time.

I don't go to look at art often enough these days, but sometimes, if I have an hour to spare, I'll sneak into the National Gallery and indulge in a little voyeurism. Room 25, just past the Rembrandts, is home to the Dutch interiors – those casual snapshot glimpses of everyday seventeenth-century lives. Sometimes I wonder if, in a few generations time, people will look with the same hushed reverence at magazine spreads where so-and-so welcomes you into their lovely home. But I doubt it. The level of detail may be the same, but those photos are all about lifestyles, and the Dutch interiors are all about life. They're scenes from a drama where nothing much is happening. There's a woman dishing up some just-cooked fish in a courtyard and another sharing a drink and a little mild flirtation with two men. A third gathers the ingredients for supper with her child. They're prosaic and poetic at the same time, and part of their appeal is that women are often at the heart of them, doing practical, workaday stuff, not just luring their menfolk with apples, or naked on a bed shooting the breeze with a cherub.

If I want the full peeping Tom experience, I go to the little wooden plinth in the middle of the room. There stands a painted box with allegorical images on the outside. But it's the inside that fascinates me. If you look through one of the little peepholes you'll see another domestic interior, only this time in 3D, painted in fiendishly clever perspective for people like you and me, four hundred years later, to come and have a good nose around.

As a child I spent a lot of time in art galleries. A lot of time. My father's an artist, and looking at pictures with him is a wonderful experience – he can lead you behind the scenes of a work of art, so that you begin to understand not just the piece itself, but the process through which it came into being. But you have to be prepared to put in the hours. Go to a gallery with Dad, and you'd better expect to write off most of the day. Wear comfy shoes and maybe pack some Kendal mint cake for sustenance, because he'll know something worth knowing about pretty well everything in there – and trust me, you won't want to miss out.

I have to confess, I didn't always appreciate this. There were days when we'd walk into yet another room of eighteenth-century landscapes and I'd think: can he not, just once, say 'and here are lots more pictures of trees', and pass straight on to the café? And sometimes the sheer intensity of his passion, the way he'd go up close and peer at a particular brushstroke, and expect you to do the same, would draw a small crowd of curious tourists. They'd think he was a guide and begin to follow us around. On several occasions, he got told off by guards for craning too far over a security barrier. When you're a teenager, the last thing in the world you want is your father attracting attention to himself in a very quiet, public place.

But by and large, I relished being taken around exhibitions by my own pet expert. And though, unlike my brother, I barely remember anything worth passing on to my own children, he has instilled in me two qualities that I'll always carry around: a feeling of excitement when I walk into an art gallery, and a willingness to be open-minded.

He taught me the latter with a little help from Carl Andre. In 1976 *The Sunday Times* published an article criticising the Tate Gallery's purchase of one of Andre's works. It was called *Equivalent VIII*, but it was taken up in the popular imagination as an exemplar of everything that was wrong with 'modern art', and henceforth it would always be dismissed as 'the pile of bricks'.

In spite of, indeed probably because of, the hostile headlines and the general ridicule that followed, my dad decided that the pile of bricks was a jolly good thing. He took us to see it, and talked excitedly about its geometry, the way it brought out the beauty of everyday objects and the tradition of minimalism from which it had emerged. I'm not sure he actually *liked* it, I'm not even convinced he believed his own defence of it, but he resented the lazy simplicity that implied it was some kind of con trick. He had the same attitude towards Barnett

Newman's work and Bridget Riley's and Jackson Pollock's. The mere fact that someone might stand in front of a piece, roll their eyes and say 'I could do that', became reason enough for my dad to champion it.

Thanks to him, I've never had a problem finding any art accessible. There are those who will happily go to see Turners or Van Goghs or Leonardos, but rule out any art that might be labelled 'modern'. Much of it isn't even 'modern' any more, but that doesn't really change things. If it isn't apparent what it's meant to be, or at least that it took a certain expertise to make it, they're not interested. Not for the likes of them, thank you very much. And I think that's a shame. But I also think the art world could make life a little easier, be a bit more welcoming.

You might have heard the phrase 'I may not know much about art, but I know what I like' used by the cognoscenti to ridicule a certain narrow-minded philistinism, a lack of curiosity. It's clichéd and dismissive, of course, and that's bad enough, but worse than that, it implies that 'liking' art isn't good enough. No siree, not by a mile. You also have to 'know' about it.

This isn't much of a problem with Dutch interiors. Anybody can tell you what they're all about. You don't even need to know biblical references or mythological tropes, like you do with Renaissance art. Landscapes are similarly non-threatening. You can read about them if you want to, learn a little about sources of light and perspective, but honestly if you'd rather say 'isn't it clever the way that looks just like a hay wain', then that's fine too.

It's 'abstract' art that separates the men from the boys. You look at a Matisse cut-out or a late Picasso and think, 'Hmmm.

Now what should I say about that?' Don't you? Of course you do. Not 'how do I feel?' or 'what do I think?' but 'what should I say?'

We're comfortable with art that looks like something. But it *isn't* actually the thing it looks like. Magritte pointed that out with his 'Ceci n'est pas une pipe' painting. It looks like a pipe, sure. But it isn't one. Because it's a painting of a pipe. It's a simple statement of fact. The *Mona Lisa* isn't the Mona Lisa, and *The Hay Wain* isn't a hay wain. They're all just pretending to be what they look like. The pile of bricks, conversely, actually *was* a pile of bricks. Which makes it all the more strange that people called it a con.

As soon as you engage with modern art, you have to be prepared to adopt a position. Maybe it's the defensive one I've been taking, or the 'any idiot could do that' one that makes me feel defensive in the first place. But it's quite hard to be neutral; to just look at a thing and absorb it. Everyone – those who love it and those who hate it – conspires to stop you doing that.

All too often, when you go to a gallery, you're presented with stuff to read – screeds of information on what the artist intended you to take away from their work. I've always preferred to ignore it. I think a work of art should speak for itself. After all, when I read a book, I don't expect the author to have to explain it to me.

Music is the most abstract art of all. Save for a few bars here or there that sound like a cuckoo or a peal of bells or a marching band, everything else is pretty well up for grabs – a collection of sounds plucked from thin air, that sometimes, somehow, has the power to make you weep. Do we worry about it? Do we read fretfully through the programme notes so that we know what we're supposed to say? Not usually. Most of us are perfectly happy to let our emotions guide us through. Two people listening to the same piece of music will have totally different images going through their heads, all equally valid. Their experience of it is unique to them. That absence of right or wrong is one of things I find thrilling about all kinds of art; one of the reasons I keep coming back for more.

If I go to a gallery with a friend, I feel we have to talk about what we're looking at, and that ruins the spontaneity for me. Not only do I not want to know what the artist was thinking, I don't really want to know what my friend's thinking either. I spend my whole life dealing with words; art gives me a little break. It takes me into a world where feelings matter more. Ideally, I like to look at it on my own. If I'm there with someone else, it's harder to lose myself in it, to let it wash over me. And it's with modern art that I feel that most of all.

I thought about this a lot at the Rothko exhibition. Jane *does* know a lot about art, and a lot about a lot of things. She's an academic, and many's the time I've asked her what she's currently working on and not understood anything very much for the next ten minutes. This isn't because she deliberately obfuscates. Quite the reverse. She would never, for example, use the word 'obfuscate' where 'complicate' would do perfectly well. No, Jane communicates things as clearly as possible; it's just that what she's communicating requires more brainpower than I will, in my lifetime, be able to access.

So going round the Rothko with Jane wasn't a question of opening someone's eyes to something unfamiliar, but of going to see something that we both already loved. The fact that she was there at all meant some kind of discussion was inevitable, but we know each other so well, I was pretty comfortable that we could keep it to a minimum.

At first, the paintings were breathtaking in a good way. Enormous canvases filled with colour, like gaping holes that you could just fall into, thinking whatever random thoughts came and went around your head. But after a while, something started to bother me.

All Rothko paintings are arresting, and in the past, I'd been happy to wallow in their presence, and not to ask too many questions. But seeing so many in one place, room after room of huge floating blocks of colour, all very similar, yet all slightly different, it was no longer enough to say you liked it. You had to ask yourself why. Why had he painted so many? Why were they all so similar? What was the significance of the differences?

I kept imagining people looking at them and saying, 'I could do that. It's just a load of paint. Can't you see? The emperor's got no clothes on and here you are, admiring the tailoring.' What would I say in return? The paintings moved me all right, but I really felt, for the first time, that liking them wasn't enough. I was going to have to know about them as well.

None of this was Rothko's fault, of course. He'd done his thinking when he painted them. If I now felt the need to come up with some thoughts of my own, and was feeling the pressure to sound intelligent to my friend, that was my funeral. It's just that I hadn't expected his work to make me feel quite so ... inadequate. I mumbled a few half-baked non sequiturs: 'I think I prefer the ones where the outlines are, you know, smudgy. And that orangey red really zings out at you.' And Jane, because she's a nice person, nodded eagerly, as if these were the very insights she'd come to hear. But still I felt inadequate. If I couldn't think of anything to say about them, then why was I there looking at one after another after another. It can't have just been because I liked the colours. If it was, I might as well have stayed at home with a paint chart.

I started thumbing through the catalogue, hoping at least to leave here better informed. It was when I found this quotation from Rothko himself that my mood turned sour: 'The people who weep before my pictures are having the same religious experience I had when I painted them. And if you, as you say, are moved only by their colour relationship, then you miss the point.'

The colour was, of course, exactly what I was responding to, and it turned out it wasn't good enough. I'd come all this way to look at this man's work, and here he was, judging me from beyond the grave, telling me that even though I admired his paintings, the way I admired them was wrong. I may not have known much about art, but I knew enough to know that I didn't know enough about what I liked.

No wonder people felt alienated by the abstract; I'd been going to galleries all my life, and even I was an outsider. I looked around the room again, from one huge monolithic image to the next, like Stonehenge in Technicolor. They were magnificent. They were still making me feel small, but actually the feeling of inadequacy had passed. I closed the catalogue and put it back in my bag. It felt wrong to stand there reading about something that was staring me in the face. 'Knowing' about art is, and always will be, much less important for me than 'liking' it, or at least appreciating it. Knowing about it matters if it gets you to the gallery in the first place – and that's where my dad's teaching was so invaluable – but once you're there, you're on your own. It's between you and the work. If it stirs something – great. If it doesn't – it hasn't worked for you. Maybe it will for the next person, but it hasn't for you. And you don't need to apologise to anyone – not to your companion, not to the artist, not to yourself.

In my head, I composed a little memo to Mr Rothko. 'Dear Mark, if I may call you by your first name after seeing inside your soul for the past forty minutes. I love your paintings. Always have, always will. If I'm totally honest, I don't actually "weep before them" and I wouldn't call it a "religious experience". But I'm a fan. And seriously, you need people like me – you, the art world, I mean. Because there aren't many of us willing to give the more outré stuff a chance. Here we are, Jane and me, looking and thinking and feeling and being moved. I just hope that that's enough for you. And I really think it ought to be, because that's a pretty amazing legacy for any artist.'

I walked into the last room alone. The paintings were bleaker, the colours more monochrome and oppressive. Jane came in a few moments later and we stood together, shifting our weight from foot to foot, cocking our heads and alternately peering and squinting. But neither of us said very much. At last, she nodded her head decisively, as if she'd finally found the observation she'd been searching for.

'Bloody hell, I need a drink,' she said.

Hello, I must be going

I was leaving a crowded motorway service station early one morning clutching my takeaway coffee and anxious to get back on the road. It was cold and my shoulders were hunched as I hurried back to the warmth of the car. I was certainly frowning, possibly mumbling expletives under my breath. A trio of middle-aged men stood huddled together in the car park, smoking. As I passed them, one of them called 'good morning' to me. But it wasn't a cheery good morning. Nor was it casual, flirtatious or an automatic reflex. It was a 'good morning' with purpose, a reprimand – it said, 'You can't just walk past me without passing the time of day. I exist and I demand a hello from you.'

I greeted him back, of course, then got to my car and drove away. It niggled away at me, that 'good morning'. I felt guilty for not acknowledging this man I'd never met before and would never see again. Who was I to walk straight by another human being without a second glance? What made my preoccupations, my circumstances, my story so much more engrossing to me than the chance to nod a greeting to a stranger? If only we were all a little more friendly, wouldn't the world be a nicer place?

But then the guilt began to fade and was replaced by a tiny flicker of indignation. Hang on a second, the flicker seemed to say, that place was packed, the car park was freezing. Did he really expect every single passer-by to say hello to him? A service station is, by definition, a zone of transience, a functional hub. You go to the loo, you eat some disappointing food, you buy a neck support cushion you'll never actually use and you carry on with your journey. A service station is not a destination in itself, not a social centre. If I'd known him and walked straight past him, then yes he would have had the right to feel snubbed. But standing outside Costa Coffee on the M4? Really? That's where you're hoping to network?

Ironically, I was on the motorway that morning after a week walking in the countryside. One of the things city-dwellers love about the country is the friendliness of the people. When you go for a walk, you gleefully say hello to everyone you meet along the way. It's the done thing, as much a part of the country code as closing a gate behind you and not letting your dog savage a sheep. Everybody plays along. In the city, nobody says hello to passers-by. This is often blamed on a lack of trust, a wariness that city life imbues in you.

It may well be true that we're more inclined to let our guard down in the country, but logically, of course, it makes no sense. If you're naturally cautious but fancy trying your hand at socialising with strangers, you'd be better-advised to do so in a built-up area with plenty of people around to hear you scream, than to wait until you're on an isolated woodland track. But no, the rules are ingrained and widely understood – countryside setting, say hello; urban sprawl, head down, hands in pockets, keep yourself to yourself. Now surely ... and I'm aware that I'm obsessing over this, but indulge me ... surely a motorway service station, even one that may lie within a rural area, is nonetheless a quasi-urban construct. Surely city rules apply. Don't they?

After giving 'good morning' headspace for far too long, I decided to file it away with all the other inexplicable social muddles I've experienced, and think no more about it.

Back in London the next day, I went shopping for clothes. In every shop I went to the assistant said hello to me and I said hello right back at them. I've shopped many times, I've been a shop assistant myself, I know how these things work. Sometimes the exchange is a little more detailed – if they want to know whether you're looking for something in particular, for example – but basically that's the pattern. I couldn't find what I wanted, so I thought I'd try one more outlet before giving up.

'Good morning,' said the assistant.

'Good morning,' I replied and moved further into the shop.

'How are you today?' he continued.

I hadn't been expecting a supplementary question, but I was happy to reassure him that I was fine. It crossed my mind to ask him how he was in return ... after all, that's what you do in a conversation. But then I remembered that this wasn't a conversation, I was merely here to browse through merchandise, so I felt on balance a smile would do instead, and took a further few steps towards the rails.

'Are you having a good day?' he continued.

I winced a little. What I wanted to say was, 'Well, yes, I am having a good day. But here's the thing: you seem like a really nice bloke and everything, but ... I have friends. And I'm sure you do too. I'm just here to look at clothes. So we don't need to do this whole faux-conversational thing. After all, if we carry on with it, and get to know each other, maybe develop a real connection – who knows? – then you're going to feel a little bit awkward asking me for money if I happen to find something in here that I want to buy. Now, admittedly, that becomes less and less likely with every second you keep me standing here talking to you and not browsing for cardigans, which is – forgive me – the purpose of my visit. But it could happen. And if we take that to its logical conclusion, and we change the rules of shopping so that everybody has a chat and makes friends and no money ever changes hands ... well, the retail sector will collapse, you see, and the economy will be in a pretty parlous state. So I hope you'll understand, but for your sake and the sake of the company that employs you, indeed for the good of all mankind, I'm going to go and look at cardigans now. On my own. Rather than stop and chat with you.'

That's what I wanted to say. But remembering how guilty I'd felt at the service station for the simple misdemeanour of failing to instigate a hello, I decided instead to go for the polite option.

'Very good thanks,' I answered. And then, with a slightly audacious flourish, I added, 'And you?'

His eyes flickered momentarily. 'Fantastic,' he replied. But he didn't look like he meant it. He looked tight-lipped and faintly resentful. I'd out-friendlied him, and he had no further cards to play. I went to look at the knitwear and he left me alone while I did so. It was all very peaceful.

Now, reading this, you might think that I'm incredibly churlish. After all, how could anyone resent a person passing the time of day in an amiable fashion? Why should all communication in public spaces be transactional? To which my responses would be, I'm not, I don't, and it doesn't. I happen to like it when shop assistants are chatty. I'm lucky enough to live in a part of London that still has a high street, by which I mean it's not just a parade of estate agents and betting shops, but you can buy actual things that an actual human person might actually need. There's a fishmonger, a butcher and a greengrocer, a bookshop and a couple of nice independent cafés. Most mornings, my husband and I go for a walk and get the ingredients for that day's meals. We buy our washing-up liquid there and our light bulbs. And then we have a coffee and go home. Now the point I'm trying to make, other than to fill you in on the fascinating minutiae of our days (NB for specific recipes and recommendations of washing-up liquid brands, etc, please see exhaustive foot-notes), is that in every single one of these shops we stop and chat with the staff behind the counter. Mostly it's about the weather or some sporting fixture or whatever's in the news that day. But it's completely delightful and I wouldn't have it any other way. That little bit of conversation is so important, I wouldn't even demean it with the term 'small talk'; it's the very stuff of human existence.

So I can assure you, this isn't about me being stand-offish or aloof. It's not even about being shy and wanting to keep myself to myself. What I'm objecting to is a particular kind of pro-forma chat, passive-aggressive chumminess, the sort of hello that's actually just about reeling you in.

When I was a shop assistant, I realised pretty quickly that there's a fine line between being friendly and hassling a customer to buy. 'Can I help you?' for example, is pushier than 'let me know if you need any help'. The latter leaves it up to the customer to decide where browsing ends and buying begins. Say 'can I help you?' in the wrong tone or too soon, and you might just as well say 'what do you want and why are you here?'

When I was a student, there was a clothes shop in town where none of us could afford to buy anything. Occasionally you'd wander in on the off-chance there might be reductions, or just to remind yourself that there were high-quality clothes in the world, and not just the ones in the charity shop that smelt like someone had died in them. But the main reason to go in was to see if you could complete a circuit of the rails without the shop assistant, who could spot a time-waster at fifty paces, saying disdainfully, 'Were you looking for anything in particular, or ...?' It was the 'or' that said it all. That 'or' meant, unequivocally, 'or are you just here to clutter up my glamorous shop, you impoverished scum?' Clearly, being that unwelcoming is bad for business and just plain rude. But there's another extreme, which can be just as offensive.

There is a particular chain of high-street shops – I won't name it, but you'll know it the minute you cross the threshold – where the staff have been trained to *befriend* the customer. A simple 'hello' is not enough. From the moment you step inside, a shiny, smiling stalker will dog your every move, asking if you've shopped there before, making suggestions, complimenting your choices. Now, if you'd never in your life been shopping, and were frankly at a loss to understand how the whole concept worked, then it would be brilliant to have an expert on hand. How else would you know that an item comes in a range of colours, other than the fact that piles of those items *in* a range of colours are on a shelf right in front of you, which now I come to think of it, is quite a substantial clue? But if, like most of us, you have some prior experience, and are confident that you can make a pretty good fist of the whole looking-at-things-and-asking-how-much-they-cost game, then this high-level interference is truly off-putting.

On one occasion, in the brief time between my daughter handing over her pocket money for something and the assistant putting it in a bag, a song had come on the radio which the assistant told us was her favourite.

'Oh my God, this just makes me want to dance,' she proclaimed, and as if to prove it she did, right there behind the counter, for the whole duration of the track, while my daughter stood there with her hand outstretched waiting for what she'd bought so she could go home. Now that's not customer service, that's weird. It's as if they'd handed the responsibility for staff training to some doomsday cult. Somebody, and on a hormonally imbalanced day it might just be me, needs to explain to the people who enforce this guff that it is counter-productive, that we're all not all guests at some teenage pyjama party, that we as customers reserve the right to be reserved.

One of the first comedy sketches I learned by heart was a monologue written and performed by Alan Bennett and consisting of an unworldly, donnish man attempting to send

177

a telegram. He is continually thwarted in this by the unheard phone operator misunderstanding him. At one point, Bennett's character remarks with quiet exasperation that he and the operator 'seem to be drifting into a somewhat redundant intimacy'.

Modern life is full of redundant intimacy. There is an app that I use a great deal in my work. It's designed for actors, and it works like this: someone – my agent, a producer, whoever – emails me a script; I forward the email to the address provided within the app; I can then download the script and use it in exactly the same way as I would a paper script (highlighting it, making rehearsal notes, recording scenes and so on), but with the added bonus of not wasting paper.

It's utterly invaluable, and I can't recommend it too highly – except for one thing. When I've emailed the script to the app's designated address, I receive an automated reply telling me it's been received. But instead of owning up to the impersonal nature of the email, the programmers have decided to make it look like it comes from a well-wisher. It starts: 'Hey Rebecca, awesome news!!!' and goes on to tell me that a script has arrived – which I know, because I sent it. The whole tone is one of hysterical delight that somebody, anybody, might have thought me worthy of sending a script to. It even ends by telling me that 'everyone here', presumably crowded around a server in some warehouse in Arizona with nothing better to do than to pray for me to get work, is shouting 'break a leg'. 'Break a leg' is what people think actors say because we're too superstitious to say 'good luck'. In fact, like the euphemism 'resting', meaning unemployed, 'break a leg' is almost never used by actors any more, and exists solely for the purpose of making non-actors appear to be in the know. Anyway, this email is a harmless piece of chirpy nonsense, and it irritates the hell out of me. I feel like I'm being treated as a guileless thespian fool, too stupid to understand the nature of digital communication.

Given that I do understand the digital world, up to a point, and that I have such disdain for redundant intimacy, what – you may very well ask – am I doing on Twitter? After all, the whole notion of a social network where countless people can read and comment on your every thought and deed – through which they can make direct contact with you and tell you what they think of you and your work – and where a community of strangers behave towards each other as if they were actually friends, would seem to exemplify everything I've been banging on about hating. Yet I check into Twitter frequently, and nobody makes me do it. It's my choice. So what do I get out of it?

Twitter, in case you've never sampled it, is an amazing, infuriating, life-affirming pain in the arse. When it first began, its selling point was that you could, in 140 characters or fewer, tell the world 'what you're doing right now'. That description actually does it no favours at all, since people who don't know anything about it – and unfortunately some who do – imagine it simply exists as a way for people with too much time on their hands to inform the general public of what they had for breakfast. If that was its sole purpose, I'm guessing it wouldn't have become quite the global success it has.

Nonetheless tweets are brief, often pointless and a bit random. There are times when I look at Twitter and wonder why the hell I bother. And then, every so often, it goes and does something amazing. It may be that you've managed to make direct contact with someone you admire but have never met, or that a shared joke with a friend has been taken up by a circle of hundreds if not thousands of witty people you'd never get a chance to meet. I've seen it used as a brilliant campaigning tool; but I've also seen it forming virtual lynch-mobs. It's a wonderful way to market an idea or tell the world what you're up to, but an ever-open door to those who just want to offend and upset you.

At its worst, Twitter encapsulates everything I loathe about redundant intimacy – people who don't know you, telling you why they hate you, on a scale that never before in human history would have been possible. And it's crowded with virtual counterparts of that man in the car park, railing at strangers who don't say hello.

But at its best, it's the high-street experience that so many people no longer have the chance to enjoy. You pass through discussing the weather and the news, sharing a joke and a brief chat with people who are not close friends, but whose well-being you care about nonetheless. It's an information exchange, a means of reminding people that you exist and that you've noticed they do too.

And that kind of intimacy doesn't seem redundant to me at all.

The face I had before the world was made

Dashing around the house one morning, I glimpsed through an open door a middle-aged woman in an apron. For a fleeting moment, I was relieved: I had so much to do that day – family stuff, work calls, accounts, shopping – it was good to know that someone was taking care of the housework. Then I remembered that we didn't have a cleaner. For another fleeting moment I thought it must be an intruder or a ghost. But the reality was much scarier than any of that: the open door I'd passed was opposite a mirror.

I went back and looked again. Yep, it was me all right. What puzzled me was that only a short while earlier I had seen my reflection, looked at it critically and for quite some time as I got dressed and put make-up on, and what I saw before me now wasn't at all how I remembered it. I took the apron off, and that certainly helped a little. There was something about the shape of it that was ageing and unflattering, the way it bunched around me and changed the line of my clothes, and its faint redolence of 1960s 'housecoat'. But it was simpler than that. I looked middle-aged because

I was middle-aged. The mystery was that most of the time I didn't notice.

In my family, we often refer to a thing called 'the mirror face' – similar to 'the telephone voice', the one we all adopt when we want to sound posher or more businesslike than we really are. The key difference, though, is that the mirror face is only there to fool yourself. Mine comes from arching my eyebrows, sucking in my cheeks and pouting. It's an expression that combines confidence with curiosity, while erasing any trace of a double chin. It's the face that I wish I had. It doesn't require any manual or surgical assistance, so it is essentially still my face, but frozen in a pose I can be satisfied with. When I put my make-up on, or blow-dry my hair, or choose what clothes go with what, that's the expression I wear to look my best. And once I've done all of those things, I don't really look at myself much for the rest of the day, so I walk around believing that I genuinely, permanently look like that. It's only when I catch an unexpected glimpse in a mirror or when somebody takes a photo of me without my knowing that I realise the truth is rather different.

For a start, my face, like yours I imagine, isn't fixed. It is animated: sometimes talking, sometimes listening, yawning, eating, concentrating, laughing – each activity carries its own facial expression. Frozen in time, each one is going to present a very different image, and it's a lottery whether that image will be pleasing or not. This, of course, is the thinking behind all those magazine columns where they show a famous person looking tired and use it to suggest their marriage is in trouble. The truth is that any one of us, captured randomly on a long lens, will at different points in our day look happy, sad, anxious, eager, loving and loathing. You might look like you're angry at your partner when in fact you're worrying that you've lost your keys. You can take an eyelash out of your eye and appear to the world to be weeping. The expression on your face doesn't always mean what it appears to mean – not that that matters a jot to a tabloid picture editor.

But to complicate matters further, our faces will also, whether we like it or not, register the emotions we *are* feeling. This is one of the things that makes acting fun – sometimes your best way to convey a character's sadness is to show her looking sad, but often it's better to have her smile. Sometimes we dissemble, sometimes we tell it like it is. Sometimes we present a polished version of ourselves, sometimes we forget that we can be seen at all. As humans, we simply don't have the presence of mind constantly to monitor our expressions.

What all of this means is that for the vast majority of the time, none of us has the slightest idea what we look like. And this isn't just true of our faces, it's true of our bodies too.

At the gym I go to, there are several mirrors. The one in the changing room makes me look chubby. The one in the gym itself makes me look skinny. Now I'd love to believe that merely walking into a room full of exercise equipment can make me drop a dress size. I could spare myself all that puffing and sweating, and just go home. But first I'd have to go back to the changing room, and looking in the mirror there would start the whole ridiculous cycle up again. The truth is, I have no way of knowing which of those images of me is the more accurate. I see myself on television and, even there there's no consistency. Sometimes I look slimmer than I'd expected, sometimes fatter. Clothes make a difference and lighting and posture. I once appeared on a chat show having carefully selected a dress I'd worn before on camera and which I felt had made me look rather fetching. But the sofa was lower than I'd expected, and this had the effect of scrunching me up in the middle. When I saw it later, I looked round-shouldered and Buddha-bellied in an outfit that had a proven track record of flattering me. There is a limit to how much we can control our appearance, so logic dictates that we put our efforts instead into controlling how much we care.

The Italians have an expression: *bella figura*. Like many phrases in translation, it can mean a multitude of things, but the one I like best has nothing to do with having a good figure. It suggests a sense of pride and self-confidence. Watch Italians doing their evening *passeggiata*, and what strikes you is not that they're necessarily better dressed or in better shape than their British counterparts, but that they think they are. As a family we've become slightly obsessed with this. When you sit outside a bar in some little Italian town, you watch the locals parading up and down with swagger, and then you spot the British tourists shuffling along looking hunched and apologetic and you realise that's what *we* look like, and there's no earthly reason why we should. We too can stand up straight and walk with our heads held high; we just don't because we're too self-conscious. I have a theory that it's down to the weather – we spend so much of our year shivering that we've failed to develop the knack of a relaxed saunter. But if you try it, you'll instantly feel more confident, more glamorous, more ... Italian. And why not? I love being British, but it's exhausting using every muscle in your body to apologise when you don't even know what you've done wrong.

Bella figura is the simplest, cheapest, safest way to control the way you look. Cosmetic surgery is none of those things, and yet it becomes more and more commonplace with every year that passes. I find this utterly bewildering. I understand that none of us looks perfect – trust me, I *really* understand. That's why I wear make-up, buy control undergarments, and do my mirror face. And I understand that ageing can be hard to accept – that's why I dye my hair and reject perfectly blameless items of clothing because I feel I can't 'get away with them' any more.

I appreciate that for some people, their appearance is a source of genuine misery, and for them cosmetic surgery may provide some relief. What I'm puzzled by is this: there is an increasing assumption that invasive procedures – altering your face or your body – are no big deal, just something people do these days. I worry for the young, the vulnerable and the easily led who are buying this line that we all have to look a certain way; who are prepared to put their health at risk and spend their hard-earned money on making themselves look fashionable. Bodies are what they've always been: some are fat, some are thin, some are young, some are old. Fashion – by definition transient – should simply sit on top of those bodies, making little *trompe l'oeil* adjustments. Altering your actual body for fashion, pumping stuff in, lopping chunks off – surely that can't be right?

I'm baffled that people are so ready to accept it. Of course it's your personal choice if you want to take the risk of cosmetic surgery. But when you watch a reality show where all the women, and it is mainly women, have had so many procedures done that it's hard to tell one from another, that smacks to me of something beyond personal choice – of a kind of tyranny. They're changing their faces, their breasts, their buttocks and whatever else because it's become the norm; because if you don't, you're seen as a bit freakish. And these procedures aren't 'cosmetic'. Getting your nails done is cosmetic. Having a nose job is structural. What kind of crazy looking-glass world are we living in when perfectly healthy people are having their noses smashed in just to make them look on trend?

I suppose what puzzles me most is having that kind of certainty. I've already established that I don't have any clear idea from one minute to the next what I look like. How can anyone – in the absence of, say, a disfiguring injury – be so certain about their appearance that they know, just *know* surgery can only improve it? Do they not have a moment of doubt, as they walk through the doors of the Clinic of Illusory Beauty Enhancement, that they might just come out looking worse than they did before?

I'm no more sanguine about non-surgical procedures. Call me unadventurous if you will, but if someone came up to me and offered to inject botulism into my eye socket, my answer would be a polite but firm 'no, thank you'. Yet more and more people are saying 'yes, why not? Whip out your syringe and let's give it a go. What could possibly go wrong?'

As a non-conformist, information-obsessed hypochondriac, I suppose I'm not cosmetic surgery's ideal consumer – at least not unless desperation sets in. And on the day I caught sight of myself in the apron, it nearly did. I looked at myself, struggling to understand how I could have grown so much older without noticing it, and wondering what, if anything, to do about it.

But the answer is that I can't do anything about it. I'm getting older because time and muscle wastage and hormone changes and bone density dictate that I am. Ageing's not great, but it's better than the alternative. And I don't believe people who do smooth out the cracks and creases feel any happier than I do about growing older. They just look happier because they're physically incapable of frowning any more.

As I stared at my reflection, I tried to think Italian. I straightened up my spine, threw back my shoulders, raised my chin. Then I did my mirror face again, and the cheekbones came back and the frown disappeared for an instant. W B Yeats understood it, that need to adjust and improve. He called it 'looking for the face I had before the world was made'.

But I'm better off looking for the face I have now, the one the world *has* made. I want my face to reflect the world and the impact it has had on me. I don't want to do stuff to it that stops me showing my emotions or hiding them, for that matter. There'll be plenty of time to look plumped-up and chemically enhanced when they've embalmed me. For now, I want to wear my middle-aged looks with pride and confidence. I want to exude that *bella figura* spirit. Maybe I'll just give the apron a miss next time.

The good neighbour

Several times a day we see, passing by our front window, an old man with his dog. The man walks haltingly, and the dog occasionally strides ahead to snuffle around a bin or cock his leg up against a tree, but always obligingly comes back to his owner and slows to match his pace in a companionable manner. We took against this dog a while ago when, faced with a pile of crap on our front path for the fourth day in a row, we realised that it was responsible. But neither Phil nor I had the heart to address its owner about it, not least since the old man's difficulty in keeping up with his pet meant he almost certainly knew nothing about it. Eventually it moved on to fouling someone else's property, so the ethical dilemma of whether to ask an arthritic man to bend down and pick up his dog's mess pleasingly became someone else's to resolve. I have only spoken to him once in fact when, leaving for work one day, I closed the front door as he happened to be passing and the dog nearly jumped out of its fur. He told me off and I apologised, even though I didn't think it was entirely reasonable to expect people to leave their front doors open all day just because your pet's a wee bit nervy. But otherwise we both go about our business with a nod or, in my case, the occasional unanswered smile.

One morning, Phil and I were leaving the house to go shopping and we saw our next-door neighbour Alex with her little boy. While we exchanged a few pleasantries, the old man and his dog came along. The little boy patted the dog, and the old man said something quietly to Alex. I didn't hear what it was and I don't think Alex did either, but she smiled and said, 'Look at the time,' and that she'd better get her son in the warm. At this, the old man glanced at me and Phil for a brief moment and then walked away. It crossed my mind that I probably should have asked if *I* could help with whatever it was he'd mumbled, but I just assumed it was something to do with the dog and the boy, and was therefore none of my business. So we got in our car and drove off. I glanced behind me as we turned the corner, and saw him shuffling along, while the dog squatted by a gatepost five doors down.

'Did you hear what he said?' I asked Phil.

'Who?'

'The dog man. He said something to Alex. Do you know what it was?'

'No, maybe he asked them to help him walk the dog. Probably just wants a bit of company.'

Of *course* he did. It was obvious. And I should have offered to help. It had flitted across my brain to, but I'd let inconvenience outweigh kindness. Now I hated myself. But what bothered me even more was that he hadn't actually asked us. He'd looked us square in the face and come up with a resounding 'nah'. Maybe he hadn't got over the door incident; maybe he just didn't like the cut of our jib. But I think it was more than that. I think we were exuding some kind of 'do not approach' pheromone, because frankly, we're not that neighbourly.

I don't really 'do' neighbours. I'm friendly enough on an in-passing basis, but in the day-to-day run of things, I'd really rather not get involved. Don't get me wrong, I'd be there in a crisis, helping however I could. It's just that most days aren't a crisis. Most days are days when there are a million things to do and not enough time to do them. So, if there's nothing I can help you with, and you're after anything more than a brief amiable chat then, regretfully, I'm not your woman. Your neighbours are, after all, strangers in all but geography. We're lucky enough to have some perfectly delightful ones, but it doesn't do to get too close to them, nor they to you. It's bad enough that your walls are touching, that you can hear every time they have a row, or run a bath, or flush their loo, and that they – unthinkably – can hear when you do the same. Surely that's involvement enough for anyone. I'm happy being on first-name terms, taking in parcels, looking after emergency sets of keys, throwing back lost footballs, talking about the weather. But, beyond that, I have my friends and they have theirs. There's no point getting all clingy with people, just because you have matching postcodes.

For me, the perfect neighbourly chat runs like this:

Me: Hi there.

Them: Hi.

Me: How's everything?

Them: Good. You?

Me: Yup. (Sound of engine starting.)

Sometimes, if I'm feeling especially perky, I may add a bit of colour, like 'bit cloudier than yesterday', 'kids are growing up' or 'nearly Christmas', but by and large I'm happy to leave it at that for weeks, months, even the odd decade or two. So it's no surprise that when an elderly man is on the trawl for companionable spirits, he's not going to put me on his list.

Which is a shame, because actually I would like to help. As someone who hates being alone myself, being lonely is just the sort of crisis I'd respond to. If I wasn't willing to chat with a man who may go for days with only an incontinent spaniel to talk to, then what kind of stone-hearted monster would I be? And anyway, it could prove to be a nicely symbiotic relationship, an old man and an actress: one eager for company, the other willing to talk for hours about herself.

So how could I get this across? How I could I change the image I was projecting?

I thought about putting a sign on our door:

No junk mail. No cold callers. No neighbours if only on social visits – though in extremis please ring doorbell without hesitation. Willing and eager to help. But if it's an invitation to a street party or similar, look … we'll say yes, but when it comes to it, we won't turn up. That's just the way we are. A bit antisocial. We're not bad people, but since a refusal can often offend, please don't invite us. To anything. Christmas drinks, housewarmings, birthdays, anything. Ooh, and we're not that big on Trick or Treat, either. It's basically a form of extortion, and … y'know … we're not living in America. Thanks.

The trouble was, our door just wasn't big enough.

Whenever someone commits a crime and a news reporter interviews their neighbours, you can guarantee that one of them will say, 'We didn't really know him,' before adding darkly, 'he kept himself to himself.' As if that's a bad thing. As if not hanging around outside your house endlessly bothering passers-by proves you've got something to hide.

Keeping yourself to yourself is just what you do if you've got any sense. Maybe things are different in a village, or even in a small town. But in a city, we are living – often literally – on top of each other. So it has always seemed to me that the only sane thing to do when you meet your neighbours for the first time is to say, 'This is my name, I'm here if you need me, now good luck and have a great life.'

But it doesn't always work like that. Sometimes you get drawn in without meaning to. For several years, Phil and I lived on the third floor of a block of flats. We didn't have a clue who lived next door to us or even right across the hall. We knew that there was a group of young evangelists somewhere nearby because they'd keep us up late playing gospel guitar, Strumming against Satan or something. But beyond that, it was just guesswork, and all the better for it.

One night, or to be more precise in the early hours of the morning, I woke up to hear moaning coming from the corridor. I thought I was dreaming at first, and drifted in and out of consciousness a few more times until I realised at last that it was indeed a human being, evidently in distress and just the other side of our bedroom wall. I pulled on my dressing gown and opened the front door. There in the corridor was a frail old woman in a nightie. She was staring at nothing in particular and shouting at it in German. I didn't want to scare her, so I stayed by the door and asked, in as gentle and unthreatening a voice as possible, if everything was OK. It was a stupid question really; she was around ninety and standing barefoot and confused in the freezing cold, so it obviously wasn't. I moved a little closer.

'Can I help you?' I ventured.

She turned and looked at me, and continued muttering in German.

'Would you like to go back home?' I said. I'd spotted that her front door was open, so she wasn't locked out. But I was pretty sure she lived alone, so while getting her back indoors seemed like a good idea, leaving her there definitely wasn't.

She carried on staring at me for a little, then said something abrupt and turned away again.

The early hours' fog in my head was clearing, and I realised that in between angry outbursts, she was actually counting, repeatedly and obsessively.

'Eins, zwei, drei, vier, fünf, sechs, sieben, acht, neun, zehn. Eins, zwei, drei, vier …'

I went back into our flat, woke Phil and asked him to call an ambulance. Then grabbed another dressing gown, went back into the corridor and tried to put it around her.

'Eins, zwei, drei, vier…' she hissed at me, so I folded it over my arm and gave her a bit of distance.

'Let's go back home,' I said, but she didn't respond. 'It's cold out here. Let's get you back to bed.' She looked away again, muttering at some invisible enemy somewhere in the shadows outside flat 23.

There was nothing else for it: I was going to have to do this in German. I hadn't spoken a word of it since my O-level fifteen years previously and, at two o'clock in the morning, even English was a challenge, but I decided I had to give it a go.

'Es ist kalt ...' I began, self-consciously, as if she might tell me off if I got the grammar wrong. 'Gehen Sie ...   zurück ins ... Haus?'

This got her attention. I'm not saying it made much sense to her, but it seemed to be familiar. 'Kommen Sie mit mir,' I said, trying to make it sound like a polite suggestion rather than an order which, let's be honest, can be a challenge in German.

And to my amazement, she moved towards me. I led her into her flat, leaving the door open behind me in the hope that an ambulance full of people who knew what the hell they were doing would be along pretty soon.

It was, being directly opposite our flat, the mirror image in terms of layout, so it wasn't hard to find my way to the living room. I kept repeating the few phrases I could muster, 'kommen Sie mit mir' and 'alles ist gut', until I'd got her into a chair. There was a blanket on the back of it, and I managed to put it over her knees.

'Eins, zwei, drei, vier, fünf,' she murmured.

'Ja,' I replied a bit uselessly, and then, because I really had exhausted my vocabulary, 'sechs, sieben, acht, neun, zehn.'

We went on like this for a little while, her saying a few numbers, me completing the sequence. She seemed to find it comforting, and after a while she closed her eyes. I glanced around the room. It was neat and clean and filled with chintzy furniture. On the mantelpiece there were black-and-white photographs of a wartime bride who I took to be her, young and pretty and slightly embarrassed at being looked at. There was a man who I guessed was her husband – a kindly face, sensible looking – and stern, solidly built parents or in-laws. But no sign of children. She really was alone, this woman. And she had been for as long as we'd lived here. All the time we'd been out at work and making dinner and going to the gym and watching telly, she'd been here, alone, thinking in German about people and places she no longer saw.

There was a knock at the open door, and a couple of paramedics came in. I told them what had happened, warned them that a smattering of German would come in handy, and went back to my boyfriend, my home, my life.

I never saw her again. I asked the caretaker of the block if he knew what had happened to her, and he said she'd gone into an old people's home. Some new people moved in and we never saw them either. Nothing had changed, except that I'd had a vision of how bloody awful being old and lonely was likely to be.

A year or so later, and Phil and I had moved to a first-floor flat in a converted house. There were neighbours above and below us, all very pleasant, all pretty private. It suited me perfectly.

Emma, the woman in the flat below, had a cat, and one day she popped in to ask if we'd mind keeping an eye on it while she went away for a week. She had some kind of hi-tech, mechanised feeding system and a friend to sort out water and litter trays, so there wasn't much to do. But the cat had a habit of tripping the burglar alarm off now and again, so she gave me a set of keys and instructions about how to reset it, and that was pretty much that.

The day after she left there was a ring at our doorbell. I went downstairs to find a man looking distressed.

'I'm really, really sorry. I just didn't see it. It ran out and I couldn't stop in time.'

I didn't know what he was talking about.

'I accidentally hit your cat,' he explained.

'I don't have a cat,' I said.

'Well, it came from here I think,' he said. 'Anyway, I'm so sorry. I didn't want to just drive off.'

And that's when I noticed Emma's cat lying dead on the path behind him.

'Ah,' I said. 'Right. It's my neighbour's. She's away.'

'Well, can I leave it with you? I'll give you my phone number in case ... not that I can do anything ... I just feel like I should.' He scribbled down his details and went away, leaving me with a dead cat that wasn't mine. It was a little bit messed up, but still fundamentally cat-shaped. I knew I couldn't just leave it there for foxes and birds to feast on, but I didn't know what else to do. I ran upstairs and got a carrier bag and an old tea towel. It was a souvenir of Brighton Pavilion, so it made an inappropriately jaunty sort of shroud, but I wrapped the corpse up in it, dimly aware that I'd never before handled a dead thing bigger than an insect, and that pretty soon rigor mortis would set in, which would really freak me out. Then I shoved it into the bag and took it up to our flat. I put it on the bathroom floor, since that was the room that looked most like a morgue, and stared at it.

There have been many times in my adult life when I've wished a real grown-up would come along and tell me what to do, and this was definitely one of them. I didn't want to ring

Emma on her emergency holiday number to tell her that her cat was dead. What on earth could she possibly do about it? It would still be dead when she got back at the end of the week, I reasoned, and it seemed a shame to make her miserable. But I couldn't just leave it in our flat either. I had no idea how long it would last before it started to decompose, and I didn't really feel like finding out. Maybe I should leave it in Emma's flat, but what if I she came home before I'd had a chance to warn her, and found her dead pet gaily swaddled in the hall, like some kind of warning from the mafia? I'd have to bury it, I reasoned, but we didn't have a garden. Emma had one, but what was the etiquette about digging up a virtual stranger's garden to bury their own pet? And anyway, we didn't own a shovel. It seemed to me an intractable situation. I started to get desperate: maybe I could drive the bag to the council dump and pretend I didn't know what was in it; maybe I could unwrap it and leave it half-way down the road for someone sensible to deal with; maybe I could emigrate and let Phil take it from here. We'd had a good few years together, and yes, it would have been nice to settle down, maybe have kids, give the acting career more of a go, but faced with the insurmountable obstacle of a cat corpse in a tea towel, emigration was definitely an option. Some time had passed like this, with me hovering indecisively at the bathroom door, when I became aware that I needed the loo. Since I was mere inches from it, this shouldn't have presented a problem, except that I simply couldn't lower my underwear in front of a dead cat; it seemed to me the sort of depraved act whole websites were devoted to. I had to get this thing out of my home and I had to do it now. I tried to calm down and think rationally. It was Emma's cat and Emma needed to be told. Then I could ask her what she wanted me to do.

I braced myself, practised a few times in my best 'breaking bad news' voice, then dialled the number.

'Oh God,' she said in a tone closer to irritation than heartbreak. 'He was always running into the road, I knew this would happen sooner or later. Just leave him in the hall and I'll ask my friend to come and sort it out.'

The friend, of course. I'd forgotten about the friend, the real grown-up I was hoping for who would know how to handle things.

When Phil came home, I told him what had happened.

'What did you do?' he asked.

'Oh you know,' I said casually, 'I just rang Emma and she got someone to sort it out.'

I never mentioned the hour or so panicking in the bathroom, the Brighton tea towel and the plans to run away to Australia.

I thought about all of this while I was berating myself for not volunteering as a friend to the man with the dog. About how, unless he happened to have an interest in rudimentary German mathematics, he would be better off without me; and how if I did offer to help, it might only be a matter of time before his dog was stiffening in a tea towel in my lavatory.

But I couldn't shake the feelings of guilt. I knew in my heart that saying 'I'm a useless neighbour' was actually just a cover for 'I can't be bothered to be a good one'.

Then one afternoon our friend Kevin was at the house doing some odd jobs. The door was open and he suddenly heard a voice calling for help. He went outside and asked if someone was in trouble. A man shouted that he'd had a fall in his garden. Kevin asked for the house number, said he'd be right there, and he, Phil and our son hurtled round to see what they could do.

When they got there, the man's front window was slightly open, so our son, being younger and more agile than the other two, tried to climb in. Suddenly the door of the neighbouring house opened, and there was the dog-walking old man, glaring at them, thinking they were up to no good.

'Hello,' said Phil. 'We're not breaking in, we're just trying to help the chap who lives here.'

After a little understandable reticence, he let them in to his place and allowed them to use his garden to access the one next door.

'I think he's called Sid,' he said, as they were making their way through his kitchen. 'But I couldn't honestly tell you. I've hardly ever spoken to him.'

They got into Sid's garden, picked him up, dusted him off and called a relative to come and look after him.

When they came back home, our son said, 'That's the man with the dog. I tried to pat it once but he didn't seem to like it very much.'

And suddenly a thought occurred to me. What if the thing he'd mumbled to Alex that Sunday morning (and pointedly not to us) wasn't a cry for help or a plea for companionship at all? What if he was actually politely asking a little boy to lay off his dog? I'd made a whole series of patronising assumptions: that because he was old, he must be lonely; because he was old, his life must be miserable, empty and desperate;

because he was old he was just waiting for someone like me to come along and help him fill his days. But for all I knew he may have had a loving family and a life that was a social whirl. If he'd needed me, he would have responded when I smiled at him. But he didn't. He had neighbours of his own, he knew them by name, and he wasn't mad keen on getting friendly with them either. For all I knew he felt the same as I did – that he and Sid and whoever else lived nearby would be there for each other in a crisis, but otherwise he didn't want to be crowded; that a nod and a smile would suffice, thank you very much. Not all old people are vulnerable; not everyone who's alone is lonely, just as not everyone who's lonely is alone. Maybe this man was an older version of me, and he just wanted to keep himself to himself.

The bulb of garlic

One afternoon, when my daughter was tiny, I took her with me to the supermarket. She'd spent the morning at nursery, so she was overtired, and the shopping took longer than I'd anticipated. By the time I got to the checkout, she should barely sit upright in her trolley-seat, and she was making that sad grizzling noise that toddlers make when they just can't understand why they're not horizontal. I gave her a cuddle, told her it wouldn't be much longer and promised her something delicious for tea. Then I paid, wheeled the trolley outside, and put her in her car seat while I unloaded the shopping. She fell asleep the minute I buckled her in, and I knew I'd pushed my luck. I had to get her home.

I started to pile the shopping into the boot, mentally planning my afternoon. Once she was in bed, I could make some supper, do a bit of cleaning, learn a few lines for some filming the next day ... there would just about be time for everything – as long as she had a proper nap. The tricky part would be transferring her from the car seat into the house without waking her, because if I failed, the whole scheme would fall apart.

I put the last of the carrier bags in the car and was about to wheel the trolley back when I spotted a bulb of garlic sitting in the bottom. It wasn't in a bag, just loose and alone. I remembered choosing it, I remembered putting it in the trolley – I just couldn't remember paying for it.

Now here was my dilemma – I needed the garlic for dinner that night. I couldn't leave my daughter unattended in the car to go back in and pay for it; I wasn't even sure I hadn't paid for it already. And it would have been downright cruel to wake up an overtired toddler just to check. I stood in the car park dithering for a moment or two, and then I came to a decision. I would take the garlic as a loan. When I came back to the supermarket, I'd make it up to them, but for now my daughter's happiness took precedence over the questionable status of some garlic.

So that's what I did. But the further away from the shop I drove, the more convinced I was that I hadn't paid for it. I'd committed a crime; maybe unwittingly at first, but right now I *knew* was in possession of stolen goods. My car was pervaded by the stench of 'hot' garlic. I was trafficking cloves. I found myself nervously checking and rechecking the rearview mirror – I had to be careful, watch my back. Any time now they'd be coming for me, the fuzz, the law, the rozzers. They would lock me up and throw away the key.

I got home, managed not to wake my daughter, and spent the afternoon cooking with illicit ingredients. I'd like to say the meal turned to ash in my guilty mouth, but actually it was delicious. And that in itself was evidence of my moral decline – I knew it was wrong, and still I loved it. Next stop: heroin.

The following day I was working, so my debt to society had to wait to be repaid. The morning after that I took my daughter to nursery and drove straight to the supermarket. I was on a mission. But I didn't want to go to the checkout with just one bulb of garlic in a basket – that might look peculiar. Besides we were running low on J-cloths and washing powder, and tinned sardines were three-for-two. So eventually, I joined the 'five items or less' queue – fighting the inner voice telling me to boycott it until they changed the sign to 'fewer' – and waited for my chance of redemption.

As soon as the cashier had processed the garlic bulb through the till, I asked if she could take it back.

'Sorry, love. I've already rung it through.'

'That's fine,' I said. 'I wanted to pay for it. I just don't want to keep it.'

She looked puzzled.

'The thing is,' I began, lowering my voice in case I was still somehow in breach of the law, 'I came in the other day and accidentally took some garlic without paying for it.'

'Right.'

'So now I want to pay for some without taking it.'

'OK.'

'To make it right.'

She was frowning at me, and I couldn't tell if it was disapproval or confusion.

'I've never stolen anything in my life, so ...'

'You've stolen something?' she said a bit too loudly.

'NO. No. Accidentally. So it's not really stealing. But that doesn't make it right. I took something without paying.'

'So you stole something?'

'No. Yes. Kind of. But the point is I'm paying now. I just have. If you'll take back the garlic.'

Without taking her narrowed eyes off me, she reached under the till and pressed a button.

'You'll have to talk to my manager,' she said.

And suddenly a man behind me was asking if he could be served first, because he was in a hurry, and pointing out that anyway I had more than five things in my basket, what with the three-for-two sardine offer. And the cashier said she'd let him through, which meant she had to void all the things of mine that she'd already processed, put them into my basket and hand it back to me. So I *still* hadn't paid for the bloody garlic and now the manager was on his way. Going straight was harder than I'd thought.

I waited by the side of the till, shifting from foot to foot, rehearsing my speech in my head. After a few minutes a pleasant-looking man in a suit appeared, smiled at me, had a brief whispered conference with the cashier and took me to one side.

'I gather there was a problem with some of our garlic,' he said.

'No, no problem with the garlic. Just a problem … with me, really.'

He tilted his head as if to say, 'I'm listening, not judging.' But he was actually doing both.

'The other day I came in here with my daughter. She was a bit overtired, and I paid for everything, but then I realised I hadn't paid for the garlic. It was at the bottom of the trolley.'

'Maybe it just fell out of a bag,' he suggested.

'That's what I thought too. But then I drove away and deep down I knew it hadn't. But I couldn't get my daughter out of her car seat, it just didn't seem right. And I knew I'd be coming back here, so … I figured I'd just buy another one, pay for it, give it back and you know, that would be that.'

He was openly grinning at me now.

'I'm a very honest person,' I said, as if it were a bad thing.

The manager reached into my basket and picked up the bulb of garlic.

'On behalf of the management, I'd like to give you this,' he said.

'Sorry?'

'As a gift. To say thank you for being so honest.'

'But … I haven't paid for it,' I said.

'You explained that …' he said hastily, trying to interrupt me before I told the whole sorry story again.

'No, you don't understand. I haven't paid for this one either. This was the one I wanted to pay for and give back. But then your cashier had to void the payment while I waited for you, so…'

'You don't have to pay for it. It's a gift.' He wanted me out of his shop now, I could tell.

'OK,' I said patiently, trying to clarify the situation in my own head and explain to him that he really wasn't helping.

'Here's the thing. I don't *need* any garlic – though it's kind of you to offer. I have garlic at home. The garlic I stole the other day without meaning to. It's still in good condition.'

'I'm glad to hear it. We're proud of the quality of our produce,' he said a tad smugly.

'Yes. Well … rightly so. But the point is, this garlic was merely functional; it was a substitute to be put through the till for the purposes of, I don't know … transparency. To ease my conscience and balance your books.'

'It's a symbolic garlic,' he ventured.

'Not really. It's an actual garlic. But it's here *in lieu* of the one I failed to pay for. I want to pay for it. I have to pay for it. And if I take it as a gift, as you generously suggest, then I'll still have a stolen garlic to feel bad about, and this one – because I don't actually need it – will end up going off.'

'So you don't want this garlic,' said the manager.

'No, thank you.'

'But you want to pay for it anyway.'

'Yes, please.'

He handed it to the cashier. She looked at it suspiciously as if it might explode all over her conveyor belt, then slowly typed its code into the till.

'Do you have a store card?' she asked automatically.

'No I don't have a store card,' I snapped at her, and then felt guilty about that too.

She took the money, and I heaved a sigh of relief. I thanked her and the manager for bearing with me.

'I have to say,' the manager laughed, 'I don't think I've ever come across anyone as honest as you. It's rather refreshing.'

'Well, good,' I said. 'I mean bad that you've obviously met a lot of dishonest people, but good that I'm not one of them. Oh, and one other thing …'

'Yes,' he said a little warily.

'It's "fewer". The sign. "Five items or fewer." Not "less". Sorry. It shouldn't matter, but … you know … it kind of does.'

I turned to leave, aware that he was already turning his meeting with the crazy garlic lady into an anecdote for the

Christmas party. I was almost out of the shop before I realised I was still holding the basket with my J cloths, washing powder and tinned sardines. I hadn't paid for them. This was becoming a habit.

You might say there's no question that you would have done what I did. Stealing is stealing, and you have to right a wrong at all costs. Or maybe you feel it was a fuss about nothing. It wasn't theft, because it was an accident, and making a song and dance over a simple mistake is, well, frankly a little self-aggrandising.

Perhaps you would only have returned the garlic if it'd been taken from a small independent grocers. The supermarkets are conglomerate bullies after all, out to destroy smaller traders' livelihoods. I shouldn't have been shopping there in the first place, but having accidentally nicked something, I should at least have seized the opportunity to 'stick it to the man'.

It all comes down to moral relativism, I suppose: one woman's crime is another woman's mistake and a third woman's legitimate protest. Nothing's ever clear cut. Not really.

Now that the children are older, Phil is fond of raising these questions with them over dinner. You know the sort of thing:

Would you ever kill someone?

No, never.

Not even if they'd killed someone you love?

Not even then.

Not even if they were *about* to kill someone you love?

Ah well, maybe...

What if they were about to kill someone you hate?

And on and on. Round and round until your head spins. I hate arguments like that. The fact is, I don't think you can ever truly say never – we're all capable of pretty much anything. You know it's wrong when it feels wrong to you, and that's all you have to go on. It's about instinct, gut feeling, rather like cooking. Whether you're following a recipe or making it up as you go along, you still have to use your judgement. Taste it. Trust your instinct. Sometimes you'll get it right first time, and sometimes you'll need more garlic.

Lauren Bacall stole my husband's chip

I took Phil to a swanky restaurant for his birthday. He is, let me point out, a hugely generous man, except where food is concerned. Not for him the one-pudding, two-spoons approach. His view is, if you want a thing you should order it in the first place. If, out of some misguided sense of asceticism, you choose to deprive yourself, then you can't expect him to plug the gap. Thus, anything he orders will follow a clear and inevitable trajectory from his plate to his mouth, and woe betide you if you try to reroute it towards your own.

Anyway, midway through dinner, a shimmer of cashmere and a breeze of exquisite scent brushed past our table, and when I saw an elegant hand reaching down to swipe one of Phil's chips, I fully expected him to spear it with his steak knife. But instead, he gazed upward with a serene smile at the retreating form of Lauren Bacall. I'd like to have put his passivity down to shock, but the fact was that there was one rule for screen goddesses and another rule for the mother of your children. It was his birthday, and I didn't want to start a fight. So I tried instead to pretend that I had planned the whole thing as a surprise, and the more I thought about it, the more amazed I was that no one had come up with it before: thrill your loved one by getting a celebrity to whip some food off their plate – the chip-o-gram, I suppose you could call it. The truth was, though, that Ms Bacall – Betty, as I feel I can call her now that she's on such intimate terms with my husband's dinner – had clearly learned from her long years of fame that whatever a star says or does, however bland the comment or trivial the gesture, they're providing a snapshot that we ordinary mortals will treasure for the rest of our lives.

If you're a star of that magnitude, just the fact of your being somewhere is worthy of comment – think of those columns in magazines devoted to sightings of the famous in a car park or a public toilet. When you look at it logically, a movie star, like the rest of us, is likely to be somewhere pretty much all of the time, so it's a wonder we're surprised when we see them. But we're obsessed with celebrity, and if we can't have it, then washing our hands next to someone who does will do very nicely thank you.

This spreading of reflected glory must be one of the benefits of great fame – along with the money and the fawning and the never having to travel by bus. The downside, I imagine, is that the opposite is also true. Merely by being in the same room as someone, a star can reduce that person to incoherent jelly. Being an actor, I get to meet famous people pretty often, and being an idiot, I frequently respond badly. After the first performance of a Stephen Sondheim musical I was in many years ago, I was introduced to the composer, something of a hero of mine. Unfortunately my director, who made the introduction, mentioned that I also write songs. Politeness demanded therefore that Sondheim (legendary lyricist of *West Side Story*) had to talk songwriting with me (author of some comedy ditties for Radio 4).

'So what's your starting point for a composition?' he asked me.

I blinked at him.

'What's your process?' he persevered, charmingly pretending to be interested. I was tongue-tied with terror. I have no process; I can't even read music. I suppose I could have talked to him about the practicalities: that I compose using a child's glockenspiel because it has the notes written on it, and that way I know what key I'm in; that it has one round beater and one square one that my brother made me in woodwork classes when I broke the handle off the original by trapping it in the lid. But he hadn't asked me about equipment; he'd asked about my process. This was professional chit-chat from one composer to another. He was elevating me to his rank. What could I possibly say about my process that would make Stephen Sondheim rub his chin and say, 'Wow, that's really interesting! I must try it myself some time'?

I said the only thing I could think of: 'I ... er ... I mean ... y'know ... it's like ... kind of ... crosswords.' But I said it less coherently.

'Crosswords? Hmm. In what way?' the great man persisted.

'Well ... sort of ... not many words ... y'know, to get your ideas ... across ...'

'Crosswords?' he repeated. I think he did rub his chin, but in a way that suggested bafflement rather than awe.

'Yes,' I said, quaveringly.

'In that ...?' he ventured. He really wanted to help me out here. 'In that there are parts blanked out ... in your head ... that you need to fill?'

It was my turn to look confused.

He tried again to articulate what he thought I was failing to. He said something along the lines of, 'You know the ideas that you want to convey, and the structure of the song imposes a grid which both enables and inhibits your expression?'

Which made a far better point about songwriting than I ever could have, and yet wasn't what I'd meant at all. And then the realisation struck me.

'Sonnets,' I blurted.

'Sonnets?' said Sondheim.

'When I said crosswords, I meant sonnets.'

'Right,' he replied, and did that thing where you pretend you've spotted someone over the far side of the room and leave. And I couldn't blame him. He'd more than fulfilled the duty of a famous person. He had given me a moment in his company that I will never forget, however much therapy I have.

Now it would be disingenuous of me to ignore the fact that acting has not only brought me close to the famous, but closer to *being* famous than if I'd carried on working, as I used to, in a perfume shop. But I'm a million miles away from Lauren Bacall's high-class scavenger status. The thing about fame is that when you think about it, and it seems as though we do little else these days, you imagine it to be a clearly defined state. You're either famous or you're not. But the fact that people so often ask me and other actors I know if we are famous, when clearly if we were they wouldn't need to ask, shows that the reality is much more complex. There are people who are 'names' and people who are 'faces'. You're a name if you're Michael Caine, but a face if you were that one who was in that film with Michael Caine. There are stars whose celebrity nobody questions, and celebrities whose fame nobody understands. You can be famous to one person, and not to another, depending on whether they happen to watch your kind of show or listen to your kind of music.

Fame is oddly site-specific. I can feel 'famous' in one place but be anonymous everywhere else. Since playing a politician in a show much beloved of real politicians, I've discovered that if I feel like being stared at, I can go and hang around in Westminster. I once innocently walked into a pub near Downing Street, having arranged to meet a friend there, and it was like one of those moments in a Western when the outlaw walks into the saloon and everyone stops talking and just looks. Yet I could on that same night have gone into any other pub in the country and gone totally unnoticed. I know this is the case since I still find it impossible to get served, even if I'm the only person standing at the bar.

That it's a transient state is obvious, in that you can drop out of the public eye at any time. But what is less apparent is that you can literally be famous one minute and not the next. Let me explain. Every so often, if you're in a programme that's nominated for an award, say, you have to do the red-carpet walk of shame. That's what it feels like, anyway, because unless you're at least a face, and better still a name, you won't see a single flashbulb aimed at you. To the massed ranks of photographers you are merely a chance to change lenses. Yet you still have to walk the damn thing, looking as if you really don't mind, as if you were hoping not to be recognised, because tottering down a brightly coloured rug in your best togs is what you do when you want some quiet time. But inwardly, no matter how much you profess not to care, it rankles. Once, after many years of scuttling towards the entrance head down, feigning conversation with the person behind me, I was pleasantly surprised when my arrival was greeted with a barrage of calls of 'Over here, love'. I obliged by looking their way with a modest, yet cheekbone-enhancing smile. 'Over here, love,' the calls continued, getting louder and more insistent. So I stood still, trying to remember that pose you're supposed to adopt that makes you look like you have endless legs and tiny hips, rather than the other way around. 'Move over here, love,' a photographer shouted with some irritation this time, 'you're blocking Honor Blackman.'

So when, some years after this, I was nominated for an award myself, I approached the walk of shame with my usual dread, assuming that it would be the same old humiliating ritual. What I had innocently failed to realise is that the whole red-carpet thing is managed by PR people. The photographers know who to shout for because someone tells them. Obviously if you're a face or a name, they don't need to be told, but in the case of someone like me, if you're a nominee somebody with a walkie-talkie will surreptitiously announce you in advance, because you're suddenly part of the story. So for the first time, I was expected. They called my name, I tried the pose, they took a few pictures and then a PR person led me inside the venue. Now it happened that I won that night, and in order to go and celebrate this unexpected turn of events, I had to run the gauntlet of another red carpet. This was a whole other ball game. I still wasn't a face or a name, but now I was a winner *all* the photographers took pictures of me. I was there for what seemed like an age, doing interviews and posing, with the award and without it – it was, I freely confess it, completely intoxicating. I went inside to the party and when I emerged, there were photographers there too. Since I had, merely two hours earlier, been the object of so much attention, I duly stopped and posed for them again. Nothing. Nada. Just the eerily reminiscent sound of lenses being unscrewed. It turns out that Warhol was pretty accurate with the whole 'fifteen minutes of fame' thing. Unlike Ruby Keeler in *42nd Street*, I'd gone in there a star and come back a nobody. It was a sobering experience.

All of this begs the question: does it matter? I'd love to say that fame's a vulgar irrelevance, but honestly it's hard to suppress a smirk and a quickening of the step when a complete stranger actually knows who you are. Sometimes it can be a tad embarrassing, when they think they actually *know* you rather than just recognising you from TV. When you're still not a name but are starting to be a face that happens a lot. People smile at you, or stare, or do a double take trying to place you. I've had a guy running after me down a street, waving and calling somebody else's name. Once in a market in the US a man came up to me and my family and asked, 'Are you folks from Utah?' We said we weren't and he replied, bewilderingly, 'You sure do look like you're from Utah.' We smiled and started to move away, but he suddenly called after us, 'Hold on, I've seen you on TV.'

The worst thing is when someone *knows* they know you, but can't quite remember where from. You have to decide how long to leave them guessing before venturing that they might have possibly seen you on the telly. The problem with this is that it feels so ... well, showy, to say, 'I expect you've seen my work. I'm an actor.' Firstly, it's entirely possible that they actually *do* know you and you've just forgotten, in which case you look like an arse. But secondly, if they agree that they haven't actually met you before, they'll follow it up by asking what they've seen you in. Like that character from *The Simpsons* who always introduces himself by saying, 'You may know me from such shows as ...', there's something pathetically undignified about trotting out your CV in the street.

The whole spectrum of being known and not being known affords ample opportunities for looking ridiculous. I went into a shop near my house one morning, and the owner, who sees me several times a week and always has a brief chat, said, 'Didn't I see you last night?' My first thought, I'm ashamed to admit, was that if something I'd filmed a long time before had been repeated, there might be a bit of money coming my way. So trying to hide the avaricious glint in my eye, I said, 'Oh possibly. What was that in?' She looked at me, puzzled by the curious phrasing of my question, and then said, 'In ... the street.' I left the shop, quietly hating myself.

Most of the time encounters with people who *do* recognise you off the telly are very nice and, contrary to what they seem to imagine, not intrusive at all. If it gives them any kind of a kick recognising you, then it probably gives you a far greater one being recognised.

There's a pragmatic aspect to consider, too. The more famous you are, the better parts you get offered. So even though I know that being truly famous would be 98 per cent loss of privacy and only 2 per cent getting into fancy restaurants without needing to book, there are times when I have to do things that will, to use agent-speak, 'enhance my public profile'.

To this end, I once agreed to go to one of those Christmas 'celebrity audience' shows. You know the kind of thing: a TV personality introduces TV clips to an audience of other TV personalities. The clips are cheap, the guests are free, and the broadcaster can guarantee good viewing figures because it's Christmas and nobody can be bothered to find the remote control. When I got the invitation I was, I confess, flattered that my name was even on that kind of list. And it was a 'plus one', which meant a night out with Phil, so I saw no reason to turn it down.

When we arrived outside the studio, a hassled woman with a clipboard had to check everyone's invitations. The fact that this took so long should have rung alarm bells. If the guest list was as star-studded as had been suggested, surely they wouldn't all need to have their identities confirmed. I don't imagine George Clooney has to blow his hands warm while someone asks him if he has any form of ID.

Once we got inside, I looked around to see who was there. I'm as happy to rubberneck as the next person, and it's always fun to say that you spilled Piers Morgan's drink or that Ronnie Corbett trod on your foot. But the mere fact of my being on the guest list should have given me an indication of how low-rent an affair this was. There were more dancing weather presenters than you could shake a stick at, and no shortage of people who are famous for telling other people that their houses are dirty and their children obese. If you'd wanted advice on interior design you'd come to the right place, but there wasn't much in the way of what you might call stars. I did bump into one very gifted young actress of my acquaintance.

'Hey,' I said, delighted to recognise someone at last, 'how's it going?'

'Not great. I'm between jobs at the moment,' she replied, and carried on serving cocktail sausages. At this point, I began to despair of what this evening said about the state of British culture, and what it said about me that I'd hired a babysitter to be there.

We were all eventually ushered through to the studio so that recording could begin. Phil and I found our allocated seats: front row, centre – pretty impressive; stuck behind the presenter's monitor – not so good.

You go to these things to see and be seen; if there's no one you want to see, and no chance of getting on camera, it starts to look like a waste of an evening. But in fact something very significant was about to happen. An official-looking man with a headset came over and suggested that we might like to move to get a better view. Also there was a gap in the middle that they needed to fill. A minibus full of ordinary people from an ordinary town, who'd been in a documentary about how ordinary they were and consequently become very famous indeed, had got stuck in traffic.

We stood up and began to move when someone else in a headset asked us where we were going, I explained that we'd been asked to fill the empty seats. 'Who told you to move?'

she asked. I said I didn't know his name but he looked official. 'Do you actually have seats?' she barked, as if people were forever walking in off the streets in evening gowns and lip gloss and getting past four security checks just in the hope of meeting a daytime-TV money expert. Before I could lose my temper, Phil stepped in. 'Actually, don't worry,' he said as she stood scanning the list of names, doubtful that we could possibly be on it. 'I know exactly where we should be sitting.' He took my hand and led me out of the studio. Where we should have been sitting was at home on the sofa eating a takeaway; and thirty minutes later, we were.

That night taught me a valuable lesson: if you need to be surrounded by celebrities to confirm your status, you probably want to take a good long look at what you've turned into.

Being famous isn't an end in itself. It may get you more of the things you want out of life: better job opportunities, more money, posh nights out. But it won't (or it shouldn't) make you feel you deserve them. When children say that they want, more than anything, to be famous, I wonder if what they really mean is successful. But you can be successful in countless ways that don't include fame. Or perhaps they mean they want to feel validated, envied or loved. Well, I'd argue that only the last of these is worth putting real effort into.

Fame gives you a certain power, I suppose, and if you're smart you'll use that judiciously, not by throwing your weight around but by putting it behind things that matter. But take it from someone who's been famous for whole moments at a time, fame is like going through an unexpectedly mild patch in a swimming pool: it fleetingly bathes you in a warm glow, then makes you feel a little bit grubby. Of course it must be glamorous to be one of the Bacalls of this world. But it must also make it damned difficult having a drink with your mates, popping to the chemists, buying underwear. It must mean forfeiting a normal life. And that seems an awfully high price to pay for a free chip.

How can I help?

It was nearly Christmas. London was frosted and twinkling with fairy lights, and in my head, as I walked to the theatre through Covent Garden, I was in a Hollywood movie. I was Meg Ryan, looking cute as I dragged an oversized Christmas tree to my New York brownstone apartment. Life felt good. So, naturally, I set about spoiling it.

Whenever I think things can't get any better, some tiny part of my brain decides to wipe the smug look off my face. It comes from watching too many TV dramas, I think. It's always the guy who kisses his wife and tells her he's the luckiest man around who gets flattened by that runaway train. So I begin to write my own disaster narrative. Firstly, I'll develop some 'symptom'. It may be partially real, it may be entirely imagined, but pretty soon I'm utterly convinced it'll be the death of me. I'm still in a film, but now I'm Julia Roberts in *Steel Magnolias*.

Secondly, the guilt kicks in. I look around at all those who aren't so lucky, starting with the other actors who wanted the part that I just got, moving on to the people who couldn't afford the meal I just ate. Eventually, it's all my fault. Everything. Even if I haven't actually *caused* this world of pain, then I certainly haven't done enough to make it better.

So I carried on walking down Long Acre but now I hated myself. 'Look at you,' my internal monologue sneered, 'on your way to the *theatre,* to do your *matinee* – you think you're on top of the world, don't you? But look at the world you're on top of. Look at the filth and the squalor and the poverty. What are you doing about that, eh? How are you going to make that better? Hmm? Are you going to *act* away the injustice? *Dance* poverty into history? Are you? Really? You make me sick.'

As I turned the corner, I passed a homeless guy I'd seen there every day. He just sat, impassively, in the bitter December cold, asking for money and clearly not expecting to get any. I stopped and reached into my bag. But then I remembered something: that morning on the news, I'd heard a woman from a charity saying that giving money to people on the street wasn't the best way to help. Sure, it made the giver feel better about themselves, but it was never more than a temporary boost to the recipient. Far better, she claimed, to give your money to an organisation that could help that person to get off the street; to find shelter and food and eventually work and opportunity. And if you really felt the need to do something spontaneous, then perhaps – this woman had suggested – giving some food or a hot drink would be better than just chucking a few coins at them and walking on.

I went into a café and asked for a cup of tea to take away. While they were making it, I browsed the cake section for something wholesome and filling. I settled on a flapjack.

Anything that takes so much effort to chew must, I reasoned, give a high yield of energy in return. I paid for both and headed back the way I'd come.

When I got to where the homeless man was sitting, he looked up and asked, with the same weary despondence, if I had any change.

'I wondered if you might like this,' I said and handed him the tea and cake.

He looked at them, a little bewildered, and then back to me.

'It's just ... I thought ... it's so cold, and ... anyway ... hopefully that'll warm you up a bit,' I said, trying not to sound as patronising as I felt.

His expression didn't change, so I walked away. I'd only gone a few steps when I heard him shout 'hey', and I turned around, smiling. But he didn't smile back. He just waved the plastic cup at me and yelled, 'There's no sugar.'

I want to help people, I really do. I just don't have any idea how. I give money, I do fun runs, I sponsor friends, and it all seems a bit like giving money to the homeless – probably more about making me feel better than anything else. Sometimes I read stories about the horrible ways people treat each other, and I think, 'Well, at least I don't do that.' I suppose if you can get through your day without kicking anyone or whacking them over the head with a baseball bat then that's something to be proud of. But it doesn't seem quite enough. An absence of malice isn't the same as the presence of good. I've met good people, really wonderful, selfless individuals and there's a difference between them and someone like me, going through life in their own little bubble, occasionally throwing a bit of bounty towards the amorphous 'needy'.

One day when I was at school, one of the younger girls was upset in the playground. My friends and I went to find out what was wrong, and she told us her mum had just been diagnosed with multiple sclerosis. I'd never heard of it before, and I got the feeling she hadn't either. It was just a scary term that was suddenly being used about her mother, and there she was crying and wanting somebody to make it go away. We really felt for her, and we decided we had to do something. So we thought up an elaborate scheme to raise money – some kind of performing showcase, I think – and went to talk to our form teacher about it.

'Well, that's a lovely idea,' she began. 'Do you know what this lady needs the money for?'

We didn't.

'Does she actually need money at all?' she carried on, and now that she mentioned it, we weren't sure that she did.

'The thing is,' she explained very gently, 'it's great to want to help people. But sometimes … we can't. By all means raise some money for a multiple sclerosis charity. But you can't just give money to someone because they're ill. She might be a bit offended.'

And not for the first time, it struck me that life was bloody complicated. Here we were being warned off doing something good because it might not be good after all.

The moral landscape got even muddier a year or so later when T S Eliot's *Murder in the Cathedral* was on the syllabus. One line burrowed into my brain and it's haunted me ever since: 'The last temptation is the greatest treason; to do the right deed for the wrong reason'. We rarely do anything 'good' without there being some benefit to ourselves. Either it makes us feel better, or look better, or both. So how can we be sure that the benevolent reasons for doing whatever it is aren't outweighed by the selfish ones; and, as long as the deed is genuinely 'good', how much does it actually matter?

Since I grew up and started appearing on TV, all this moral confusion has been put into even sharper relief. I make my living doing something I love. That alone is a stroke of rare good fortune. Now add to that the fact that sometimes you get a bit of public recognition for doing it. Even better. So if you have any kind of a social conscience at all – and I've never met an actor who doesn't – you try to use your public profile to do something for other people. Many charities are only too delighted to have patrons who are in the public eye, because it helps get attention from the press. Having a well-known face on the *Breakfast* sofa is a great way to raise awareness about a cause. So it seems like everyone's happy.

The relationship is symbiotic, and therein lies the problem. By using your 'celebrity' to promote a good cause, you're also promoting yourself. You pop up on TV and in magazines talking about whatever you're supporting and it makes you look good. Who's benefitting most from the publicity – the charity or you? It's impossible to quantify, and *because* you have a social conscience, you can't help feeling slightly sullied. You want to do good and you want to do it for the right reason, and sometimes that's a tricky thing to pull off.

I was approached a couple of years ago to get involved with a charity helping deafblind people, and I went along to a day centre to see what it was all about. It was one of the most extraordinary mornings of my life. The people who came to use the centre had sight, hearing and speech impairments of varying degrees of severity, but none that didn't make you wonder how on earth they got by at all. I mean, many of us – well, me, I suppose – feel pretty stoical turning up to work with a sore throat. But here were people, unable to see or hear or speak, learning to cook, writing poetry, painting, swimming, trampolining ... just getting on with it. And then there were the helpers, for whom every obstacle is just an opportunity for ingenuity; people with patience and determination and sheer bloody-minded optimism. It was, genuinely, an inspiration. So I wanted to help, of course I did. But what could I actually do that would be of any real value?

I wasn't going to give up my career to retrain as a helper – I'm simply not that selfless. So I agreed to do a bit of PR. The charity was running a creative-writing competition – to encourage deafblind people and their families and carers to write about their experiences. I went along and handed out some awards, read out some of the entries, met people, shook hands, shared jokes, ate the buffet, and had an absolutely lovely time. And I was treated like royalty – I lost track of the number of times people thanked me for being there. But I wanted to say to them, 'I'm the one who should be doing the thanking, because this is quite literally the least I can do. Short of not turning up at all, it's the least I can do. I'm not patient enough to be a helper and not rich enough to be a benefactor. So this, being here, reading stuff out loud, chatting and listening, is actually all I'm good for.'

Still, it made me feel great, knowing that I'd done something. So what would T S Eliot say? Had I done it for the wrong reason? Was it all about looking good, being seen to care, getting my picture in the paper? No. Not by a long chalk. Not even slightly, just a teensy-weensy bit? Well, maybe.

The alternative, though, was not doing it at all, which has to be worse.

And anyway, as human beings we're capable of having more than one motivation at a time. Almost everything we do is the product of a compound of higher thoughts and baser instincts. We do things because we can, because we ought to, because we want to, because it feels right, because it looks good – but the main thing is we do them.

So here's how the story about the homeless man should have ended. The next day I find him again. I hand him a cup of tea, a flapjack and two sachets of sugar. We get into conversation. I learn about his story, earn his trust, and help him find a place in a shelter to get him through the winter. That's how it would end in a perfect world; a world written by Hollywood.

But I didn't go back. I still bought extra cups of tea from time to time, but I gave them to a different rough sleeper up the road. He'd freaked me out a little bit, the first guy. I didn't feel comfortable being shouted at in the street. But that wasn't the only reason. The truth was that he hadn't said thank you. There are people out there – good people, selfless people – who will read this and be disappointed. I'm disappointed in myself. But most people, I suspect, would have reacted the same way. Which means T S Eliot had an awful lot of us bang to rights. I'd done a nice thing, and I wanted some gratitude. And if that isn't doing the right deed for the wrong reason, then I don't know what is.

For now

I got in the car and turned the key.

'Right. Well ... see you tomorrow.'

They smiled and waved and looked exhausted. Inside, it was all packing cases and holdalls, bin bags labelled 'charity shop' and 'spare sheets, bedroom 2' and 'rubbish'. The walls were covered in faded rectangles and empty picture hooks. As the engine started, my son took photos out of the passenger window – the last time he'd see Grandma and Grandpa outside their old house.

'Actually, can you take one of all of us?' I said, realising suddenly that this was it; I was leaving my childhood home for the very last time.

We all lined up by the front door: me, Jeremy, Mum and Dad, and posed awkwardly, arms round each other's waists, smiling embarrassed smiles. He took the photo and I turned to say goodbye again, but there was a catch in my voice. Mum noticed it and looked away. She couldn't deal with my emotions as well. Not today. She was only just controlling her own, jumbled up as they were with her memories in virtual bin bags marked 'newly married', 'raising a family' and 'having a career'. I didn't want to add to the pile, so I got back in the car, waved and drove off.

As we turned the corner, I pulled over to the kerb. I was out of their sight now and could let myself go. But first there was someone else to think about.

I turned to my son. 'Darling, I've been having to be all, you know ... and I just need to ... before I get on to the main road ... only I can't really drive if I'm ... sorry'. It wasn't exactly articulate, but he's a bright kid. He knew what I meant.

So now that I'd sorted out everybody else's reactions to my feelings, I could actually allow myself to have them. I started to cry.

Home. That house was, for most of my life, just home. Even once I'd moved away, and had a family and a house of my own, whenever I visited, I still talked about going home. My parents lived there for fifty-four years, and for the forty or so that I could remember, they'd done nothing but moan about it. They'd moved there because it was close to their parents and in a 'nice area'. But in their heads, they were living a different life. They didn't want a mansion; just a slightly bigger house, closer to London. They wanted to live somewhere bohemian, where there were cafés and bookshops and places selling pretty things that nobody really needs. Instead, they lived on a suburban road, where you had to drive to any kind of shopping centre and when you got there, you couldn't find anything you wanted to buy. And as the years passed, and the house became more and more rundown, they yearned to be somewhere easier to manage, in better condition, warmer, nearer the grandchildren. But still it was home.

It took probably twenty years for them to get around to selling it. The reasons to do so vastly outnumbered the reasons not to, but the obstacles were just too huge. Not the least of these was that their area was cheaper than the one they wanted to move into – the one where my family and my brother's and my mum's sister and their friends had all ended up. Downsizing wasn't anathema to them – it would actually be a relief to have fewer rooms to look after. But over the course of those twenty years they would occasionally get their house valued, and we'd all start trawling estate agents' lists to see what they could buy in exchange, and come up with a big fat nothing. For the price of their three-bedroom semi, they'd barely get a studio flat.

On top of that, my dad still worked. Being an artist, even more than being an actor, isn't something you just retire from. You don't decide one day that enough is enough; that it's time to put the paintbrush down and relax. After all, art is one of the things other people retire in order to take up. What hobbies would an artist do if he retired – a bit of conveyancing? A little light retail? Dad had drawn or painted every day since he was a kid; he was never going to give it up. Not only did he need a place to do it, he also needed somewhere to store all the work he'd already done. So a spare bedroom to use as a study was essential. Plus, they wanted a little outdoor space to grow tomato plants and sit on a summer's evening – that was non-negotiable. Oh, and designated parking would be good. And a second loo. And not too many stairs, now that they were past seventy.

All of these demands were entirely reasonable, but finding a place that met the criteria and was affordable and close enough to us all to make it worth the upheaval looked frankly impossible. And so it went on, year after year, with everyone wishing they could move, but nobody seriously believing it would ever happen.

It took a crisis – or at least what looked like one – for things to change.

It was a leaking pipe I think, but it could just as easily have been a hole in the roof or dry rot. The point was that Something Big had gone wrong, on a Friday afternoon in late summer, and nobody was going to be able to give even a conservative estimate of the cost until Monday morning at the earliest. It was an endless, joyless weekend. We all rallied around, of course. We offered moral support, which they gladly accepted, and financial support, which they flatly refused. We took food for sustenance, and grandchildren for distraction. But in the end, none of us could give them what they really needed – reassurance, not just that this problem would be surmounted, but that there wouldn't be another, bigger one waiting round the corner. Monday came, and it turned out that the Something Big was actually Something Not Too Bad After All, but the weekend of anguish had worked a minor miracle: my parents decided that enough was enough. Somehow or other, they were going to move.

It's blindingly obvious, but true nonetheless that when an adult spends a lot of time with their parents, they become an entrenched version of the child they used to be. That was certainly what happened to me and my brother. Jeremy is more sentimental than I am, and cautious when taking decisions.

He was wary, understandably, of putting pressure on Mum and Dad, of making them choose a place they didn't really want or chuck out something they did. But things needed to be done – you can't move a three-bedroom house into a two-bedroom flat without throwing away a lot of stuff, and anyway, you've got to find the two-bedroom flat in the first place. Which left me to fill the spaces marked 'outspoken' and 'bossy'.

I became a whirlwind of internet searches and emails and suggestions and edicts. Every conversation was stuffed full of 'have you thought abouts' and 'you really need to considers' and 'don't forgets' and 'whatever you dos'. And lists. Endless lists. And questions. My poor beleaguered parents were inundated with them, written in notebooks and on the backs of envelopes. What do you most want? What could you live without? What would you miss? Which would you choose between a one-bedroom flat with a garden and a two-bedroom flat on the first floor? Is being on a bus route more or less important than having a designated parking space? And on and on and on.

I gave them a week-by-week checklist of things that had to be done and crossed off before the next checklist would be issued. Week one, they had to clear the bookshelves in the box room; week two, start on the chest of drawers in the same room, but *only* if the bookshelves had indeed been cleared. If not, they were to do the bookshelves for the first half of week two and the chest of drawers in the time remaining. And because they're lovely people, they'd say 'thank you' and 'how helpful', rather than yelling at me that they weren't idiots and they really could figure this out for themselves. Sometimes, I'd get off the phone with them and feel proud of what a good daughter I was being. Other times, usually when I was lying awake worrying about it all, I'd hate myself for behaving like a despot. The truth was somewhere in the middle. I was being intolerable, but with the very best of intentions.

While I was busy micromanaging and fretting, it was they themselves who found a place they liked and could afford. This was a relief, both for the obvious reason that it needed to be their choice, and for the more selfish one that if I'd found it and it turned out to be a dud, I'd never be allowed to forget it.

It was lovely, and ticked pretty well every box on my 'what do you want from your new home' questionnaire. But it was small. So now, phase two of the throwing out had to begin. Fifty-four years' worth of stuff is bound to be a lot to sift through. But when it comes to interior design, Mum and Dad have always erred on the maximalist side. They're not exactly hoarders, not like those people you see on TV who haven't seen their bed for thirty years because it's covered in takeaway menus. But they're not exactly throwers either. It's one of the reasons I am the way I am. I never had a teenage rebellion. I just started throwing stuff away. Things come into our house now, and if they're not immediately useful or decorative, or beyond my jurisdiction because they belong to someone else, they're gone. Finished. Just the thought of it drives my parents crazy. My mother will often ring me mid-morning on a Sunday to ask if I've read some article in the *Observer* purely so that she can say, in an arch voice, 'Or have you already thrown it out?' She never tires of recalling the time one Christmas when I got so over-zealous about putting discarded wrapping paper straight into the recycling, that I threw away a present I hadn't actually opened. But she's right: it has become something of an obsession. When we moved into our current house, I put a moratorium on the phrase 'for now', as in 'I'll just leave it there for now'. My theory was that there was a place for everything, and nothing needs to stop off for a rest on its way there. I lost the battle of course. Children don't understand the concept of 'tidy', so you either drive yourself and them nuts, or you learn to turn a blind eye to the mess. But to this day, whenever Phil catches himself putting something down 'for now', he'll give a tiny glance in my direction and take it to where it belonged in the first place.

For all the ridicule I'd attracted, here was where my chucking skills could come into their own. Fifty-four years' worth of stuff to be filtered down to a manageable amount – if they thought I'd been bossy about house-hunting, they had no idea what was about to hit them. Every single item in that house – every plate, spoon, photograph, book, ornament, and every yellowing bit of paper – had a question hanging over it. Should it stay or should it go? The problem was that each of those items also had a story attached to it. They'd all been kept for a reason, even if that reason was only 'we'll leave it there for now'.

'It's got to go,' I would say of anything that they couldn't justify keeping. Mum would get defensive and Dad would look anxious and Jeremy would remind me that they'd bought it when they went to ... or they'd had it ever since ... And I'd sit for a moment and feel like a bitch for suggesting it. But then I'd think again of the reality of their situation, and feel the need to get steely because somebody had to. 'You won't forget things that happened just because you no longer have the physical proof. If it really means something, keep it, but otherwise ... it's got to go.'

But even as I was saying it, it sounded rather hollow. With good health and a prevailing wind, this could be me in twenty years' time, being bellowed at by my offspring in a well-intentioned attempt to clear the decks. And like my parents, I'd be nodding regretfully, and taking bags of stuff to landfill, and inwardly screaming, 'No. You don't get it, do you? It *all* means something. All of it. It might look like a receipt or a bus ticket or an out-of-date guidebook, but to me it's a shopping spree or a day trip or a holiday. And I'll never get it back. This is all that's left of it. It means so much more than it looks.'

And that's the problem with stuff: it starts out meaning something, becomes a bit pointless, sits around for years redundantly gathering dust and then, when you finally decide to get rid of it, it means something all over again. Stuff creeps up on us, like old age. We look at pictures of beautiful, minimal homes and admire their clean lines, their simplicity. But deep down we know that the only way we could live like that would be if we kept another separate house for all the stuff. We're oppressed by it, tyrannised by it. And even when we finally decide enough is enough and rid ourselves of it, we're left with residual guilt, that faint nagging voice telling you that one day, you'll be sorry; one day you'll be looking for that very bus ticket, that very book or receipt to explain some mystery, to fill in a gap in a story, and then it'll be too late.

So the throwing process was grim – but unavoidable. There was one whole bookcase full of my mum's old teaching materials. She retired years before, but saying that the remnants of her career had to be thrown away when everything from

Dad's was going with them just seemed cruel. Then there were things that they'd both held on to when they'd had to clear out *their* parents' houses – if it meant enough for them to hang on to it then, it meant something still. But there was hardly space in the new flat for Mum and Dad's belongings, let alone for their mums' and dads' as well. We spent days like this – tackling one item at a time, taking some decisions, deferring others for when we had more strength to tussle over them, winning some battles, losing others.

And finally here we were. There was still too much, we all knew that, but we'd done all that we could to whittle it down. And as Mum said, they'd have landfill and charity shops in the new area too.

We'd focused so much on the stuff, that none of us had really thought about the house itself, the fifth member of our family. The bannisters my brother had taught me to slide down; the garden where Dad had taken the stabilisers off my bike; the kitchen where Mum had taught me to tap dance; the bedroom where I'd opened my A-level results. Every room meant something different to each of us. And if there was no taking any of it to the new home, there was no leaving it behind either.

I didn't cry for long. As soon as I started, it felt like a gesture, something I was doing because I'd expected to, not because I really had to. The truth was, I wasn't sad, I was relieved – relieved that Mum and Dad had found a nice new home, relieved we'd got rid of so much stuff, relieved I would have my parents close to me again. The fact that I'd never go back to that house again hadn't really sunk in, but I felt it should have done. So I was crying more out of propriety than anything else. It seemed wrong not to.

After weeks of treating my parents like children, it was my son's turn to do the same for me. He was fourteen – gentle, kind, thoughtful, but fourteen nonetheless. No teenage boy is going to feel comfortable seeing his mum cry. He looked at me askance for a moment, let out an involuntary noise that was meant to say 'poor you' but actually meant 'oh god', then seemed to dredge up some muscle memory of what we used to do to comfort him when he cried. He reached out his hand and stroked me stiffly on the arm. Just once. Shoulder to wrist. Then he looked at me again like I was a piece of litmus paper and he was waiting to see if I would turn blue or not.

I stroked his arm back.

'I'm OK now. Thanks. And sorry. Right, let's get back to our own … to our … let's go home.'

More like a snail

When I was a little girl, the BBC would often show a short film, in between programmes, about a magical place called Evoluon. I now know it was essentially an advert for a science museum in the Netherlands, but each time it came on my brother and I would watch it all over again, relishing the shimmering, high-tech future of which it offered us a glimpse.

Seen against a Sixties soundtrack of bongo drums and celestial harmonies, the building looked like the lair of a Bond villain. Inside it, earnest young men in suits blew into metal tubes for no apparent reason. They prodded buttons and when something lit up or moved in response, nodded sagely as if that was exactly what they had expected it to do. Women in horn-rimmed spectacles and matronly dresses, who looked elderly but were almost certainly younger than I am now, wandered around puzzled and out of place, marvelling that by some stealthy revolution, they were here peering at electronic gadgetry, rather than stuck in the kitchen getting their husbands' tea on the table.

It was dazzling and different, and watching it filled me with excitement. And yet I knew with some certainty that I would never, ever go there. Because for all its allure, Evoluon was 'abroad', and 'abroad' was a place to which I had no desire to go.

I decided very early on that travel was not for me. It wasn't that I had no curiosity about other places – I loved reading and watching films, I was intrigued by different landscapes and other people's lives –I just didn't want to have to leave home to find out more. Home had everything I needed. Mum and Dad and Jeremy were there, my doll Louise, my books, my bike, my roller skates – if I went abroad, I'd have to leave them all behind. I had an inordinately strong umbilical bond not just with my family, but with home itself. You could be forgiven for thinking therefore that our house must have been luxurious, that I was scared of being without my creature comforts. But in fact, by the suburban standards of the day, it was pretty basic. We had no central heating for one thing, so during the winter months we'd routinely wake up to find frost patterns *inside* the bedroom windows. We never had a second car or a washing machine or even, for goodness sake, a SodaStream. But I loved being where I was, with the people I was there with, doing the things we did. That was all I needed.

For the first decade of my life, since there wasn't a huge amount of money around, foreign travel wasn't an option anyway, so my reluctance went unchallenged. I wanted to stay at home and, luckily for me, we had to.

The truth was, of course – as in so many areas of my life – that I was scared. I couldn't use tubes, didn't like trains, boats made me seasick, cars made me carsick, and if I ever got on a plane, I was pretty sure I wouldn't like that either. So I never did school trips or foreign exchanges; I just stayed at home reading about the world, watching films like *Evoluon* and dreaming that one day someone who worked in a place like that would invent a way in which you could travel round the globe taking your entire house and family with you.

The first time we went abroad was when I was eleven. My grandfather had died and left Mum a small amount of money. When she was a child, he'd loved taking her and her siblings on driving holidays around Europe, so it seemed appropriate to spend the money doing the same with us. For three weeks we took to the road. We ate chips with mayonnaise in Belgium, saw fairytale castles by the Rhine, had our car broken into in Amsterdam and got into muddles with my schoolgirl French. Had I known a little more about geography, we could have actually gone to Evoluon; we can't have been more than thirty miles away from it. But even without the heady rush that would surely have provided, the holiday was a proper adventure. And the truth was, I couldn't wait to come home. Even though the people I was closest to were right there with me, I can still remember feeling dislocated.

So, clearly, home for me wasn't just about family. It was about what was familiar. And increasingly, I suspected that this wasn't something to be proud of.

As I got older, all my friends started to talk enthusiastically about travel. To them, apparently, it wasn't – as it seemed to me – a thing to be avoided at all costs. They wanted to study languages so that they could spend a year abroad. They planned to go interrailing, or work as an au pair, or teach English as a foreign language. And I couldn't think of anything

I'd like less. Obviously, somewhere along the way, I'd missed out on the life lesson that travel would broaden my mind, and skipped straight to the one about all the terrible things that could happen to a person a long way from home. I tried to envisage it being enjoyable, but all I could picture was me explaining to some hostel owner in Lima what vegetarianism meant, or struggling to ascertain from a train guard how many rail tunnels there were between Warsaw and Krakow. The road to independence, freedom and adventure was full of obstacles of my own making. And it would undoubtedly have remained impassable had I not met Phil.

Phil was, in many ways, the very worst person for a girl like me to hook up with. He'd spent great chunks of his life, prior to meeting me, teaching in the Middle East, or island-hopping round Greece, or backpacking through Sri Lanka. If you asked him where home was, he genuinely had to stop and think about it – was it where he was born, or where he'd been for the past six months, or where he had ambitions to go to next? And once we were going out together, it was pretty clear that he wanted me to travel with him.

At first, the obstacles remained firmly in place. He booked us a week in Florence, and I, being too afraid to get on a plane, said we'd have to go by train. This was particularly self-defeating, since not only did we spend considerably more time travelling than we did sightseeing, but the journey also took us through one of the longest rail tunnels in the world. So I decided I'd better conquer my fear of flying.

What followed was a war of attrition. Phil would book us tickets to go somewhere. I'd start low-level worrying about the journey from the moment he booked it, building to a rabid crescendo in the days before we travelled. But we'd go, and we'd have a lovely time, and it was never quite as bad coming back – because I was heading for home, I suppose. And thereafter, I'd breathe a sigh of relief that I wouldn't have to go through all that again; that he couldn't possibly expect me to suffer like that any more. But – almost as if he'd forgotten the anguish I'd put us both through – he'd go and book another trip. He was taking a calculated risk of course, that the more often we did this, the easier it would get. Well, he got that wrong: flying stayed every bit as hard for me for the first ten years or so of our relationship, but the point is, I did it. So in that sense, it was a triumph. And when the children came along, the thought of them flying anywhere without me was so much more horrific than the thought of getting on the plane with them, that my fear started to ease off altogether. We flew long-haul to New York and Los Angeles, and because I was adamant that they shouldn't sense my anxiety, I smiled and watched films and read stories to them as if I was a normal, relaxed traveller, rather than someone who'd spent the night before praying for fog to ground all flights so that we could just stay home.

Getting to places was, of course, only part of the problem. I now had to learn to enjoy being 'away'. But one crucial discovery helped me with that.

It turned out the world was breathtakingly, brain-achingly amazing. I knew that, intellectually, of course. I'd read all those books and seen all those documentaries. But none of that had taught me what the spice bazaar in Istanbul smells like, or how it feels to watch a minke whale just feet away from your boat in Puget Sound. All the close-up photography in the world won't tell you what it's like to hang off the outside of a cable car careering down San Francisco's vertiginous hills; nor how eerie it is to see a statue of the Virgin Mary paraded at midnight through a small Italian town.

It turned out that I loved travelling; or at least, I loved some bits of travelling and I loved having travelled. Given the choice, I'd still have opted for that magical way of taking home and everything familiar with me. Staying in an apartment or a hotel – even on occasion quite luxurious ones – always feels a little like an endurance test to me. There's something about having a shower in your own bathroom at home – even if you do have to keep knocking the pipe sporadically to clear that airlock – that is more relaxing than a soak in any roll-top hotel bath. But I've learned to accept that that's just the way I am. Home for me is a complex idea. It's not just 'where the heart is' or 'anywhere I hang my hat'; it's proximity to my family and being understood and knowing what to expect.

Being with Phil has given me an insight into travellers: they're a little like snails. They carry their sense of home about with them. Everything they need to make them feel comfortable, in the deep sense of the word, is right there inside them. I used to think that to be a seasoned traveller you had to have all the right gear: rucksacks and hidden zippy money belts and tubes full of laundry gel. But what you really need is the ability to be fully present wherever you are. It's ironic really: you think of people with wanderlust always having a yearning to be somewhere they're not, but to be a successful traveller, you have to be contented wherever you are. And that's what Phil's like. Everywhere he goes, he's home.

Me? I'm almost never completely at home. If I'm with my family but not in my house, I feel displaced. If I'm in my house but not with the family, I feel lonely. Even sometimes when we're all in the house together, I can still be a little askew, because my mind is elsewhere. Home is circumstantial, dependent on externals. I need to find the inner resources to carry my sense of home around with me – I need to be more like a snail. But for now, the fact that I travel and get so much out of it is a source of enormous pride. I could easily have given up trying; I could have decided that in the absence of a shell, I'd live out my life as a slug. But I haven't and I won't. And one of these days, in defiance of my younger self, and to celebrate this world of new possibilities, I may put on some horn-rimmed glasses and a matronly dress, and go and prod buttons in Evoluon.

Acknowledgements

I owe a huge debt of gratitude to my agent, Charlie Campbell at Ed Victor Ltd, and my editor, Bea Hemming at Weidenfeld & Nicolson. Without their gentle persuasion and clear direction, I would quite simply never have written a book. At all.

Although these stories are true, I have changed the names of most of the protagonists, partly to preserve their anonymity, and partly to stop them complaining that that's not exactly what they said, that they would never split an infinitive like that and that the cardigan I referred to was blue with a green trim, *not* green with a blue trim. I hope they'll forgive me if I don't recall things the way they do, and I thank them wholeheartedly for providing me with a dramatis personae.

My wonderful parents and my fantastic brother deserve my thanks, not just for letting me write so much about them, but for their unending love and support.

But most of all, I thank Phil. He listened, suggested, guided, chuckled, rolled his eyes and never censored. Not only that, but he cooked too. My gratitude is endless.